Reminiscence Writing, Speaking, and Storytelling as Memoirs Therapy

What's the Greatest Lesson You Learned from Life?

You also could write (in your own language) a kōan (公案) (Chinese word) that emphasizes cultural criticism and theory. A *koan* is a paradoxical anecdote or riddle without a solution, used in Zen Buddhism to demonstrate the inadequacy of logical reasoning and provoke enlightenment, according to English Oxford Living Dictionaries (https://en.oxforddictionaries.com/definition/koan)

Table of Contents

How to Refresh Your Memory by Writing Salable and/or Personal Memoirs for Time Capsules

Introduction:

Chapters:

1. What's the greatest lesson You Learned from Life?

2. Writing Your Life Story or a Biography as a Play or Skit before You Write it as a Novel

Intergenerational Writing as Commitment to Values

3. What Makes a Life Story Highlight Salable as a Play or Skit?

4. Writing Plays for High-School Students, Families, and Mature Adults from Life Stories and Personal Histories: Working with the Evidence

5. What Makes a Personal History or Life Story Highlight Salable as a Play or Skit?

6. "Celebration of Life" Plays and Skits Based on Interviewing and Recording Personal Histories

7. Before Video Recording Life Stories of Older Adults: Questions to Ask

8. Life Story Plays as Dialogues with the Higher Self

9. Offering Life Stories to Audiences

10. Stories with Central Issues: Plays, Skits, or Stories with Current Events or Social History

11. How to Restore, Recover, and Adapt Diaries into Plays or Skits

12. Interviewing Techniques for Video biographies:

13. Steps to Take in Gathering Life Story Highlights to Write into Plays or Skits

14. How Accurate Are Autobiographies, Biographies, Personal Histories, Plays and Monologues Based on Life Stories?

15. Reminiscing Your Memoirs or Life Story Highlights with Animation

16.   Turning Life Story Vignettes, Plays and Skits into Computer and Board Games

17. Stimulating and Enhancing Memories: Does Writing Your Life Story As A Play for High-School Students or Older Adults Help Refresh Memories?

18. Why Reminisce Therapeutically or Write Personal Histories/Life Stories to Stimulate Memory and Build Your Own Dialogue Mirror Using Multimedia?

Appendices:

A. Ethnic Genealogy Web Sites

B. Genealogy Web sites (general)

C. Action Verbs for Communicators

\#

Introduction:

Tired of analyzing puzzles to build brain dendrites and stimulate your memory? Try writing for health—writing salable memoirs for popular magazines to enhance your memory. On your way to maturity, what have you given up? What have you added? Is your life story about disconnection and keeping your mouth shut? Or is it about connections and sharing meaning through communication?

How secure, stable, and steady is your sense of self as the seas crash around you? To what portraits will your memoirs give voice as you cross over to each new stage of life? To what in your life story will you pay tribute? Describe your watershed in colorful words, sounds, or pictures.

Readers reach out to you. Let's hear or read about your crossroads and paths taken. And to put your words to use, consider writing salable anecdotes and life experiences for popular magazines. Your social history is part of pop culture. Reminiscing is good for your memory and personal history.

Memoirs are excerpts and highlights of significant events in your life. They can be written in prose form or as a skit, play, dialogue with a relative, or as a monologue. Parts of your life story can even become material for stand-up comics in a laugh-for-your-health workout. Or you can write salable memoirs and put direct experience in a small package and launch it worldwide.

Write your life story in anecdotes of 375 to 1,500 words. The difference between memoirs and autobiographies is that memoirs are excerpts or highlights of a life story. Autobiographies are life stories than run chronologically from birth to maturity.

Write salable tributes, eulogies, and highlights of life stories and personal histories for autobiographies. Then condense or contract the life stories or personal histories into PowerPoint presentations and similar slide shows on discs using lots of photos and one-page of life story.

Collect experiences. Flesh-out news stories, linking them together into first-person diary-style novels and books, plays, skits, or other larger works. Write memoirs or celebration-of-life tributes for the living.

If ghostwriting is too invisible, write biographies and vocational biographies, success stories and case histories, and customize for niche interest groups. Your main goal with personal history and life stories is to take the direct experience itself and package each story as a vignette.

The vignette can be read in ten minutes. So fill magazine space with a direct experience vignette. Magazine space needs only 1,500 words. When you link many vignettes together, each forms a book chapter or can be adapted to a play or script.

By turning vignettes into smaller packages, they are easier to launch to the media. When collected and linked together, they form a chain of vignettes offering nourishment, direction, purpose, and information used by people who need to make choices. Here's how to write those inspiration-driven, persistence-driven life stories and what to do with them. Use universal experience with which we all can identify.

Included is an excerpt from a full-length diary-format first person memoirs novel and an entire three-act play. Also, there is a monologue for performances. There's a demand for direct life experiences written or produced as vignettes and presented in small packages.

Save those vignettes electronically. Later, they can be placed together as chapters in a book or adapted as a play or script, turned into magazine feature, specialty, or news columns, or offered separately as easy-to-read packages.

If you are working with activities directors and persons with dementias on stimulating memories, I highly recommend reading an online article and viewing the resource links at the Web site called, About Health & Fitness at: http://alzheimers.about.com/cs/treatmentoptions/a/reminiscence.htm?once=true&. See the article titled, *"Reminiscence Therapy and Activities for People with Dementia,"* From Christine Kennard, *"Your Guide to Alzheimer's Disease."*

#

Chapter One

What's the Greatest Lesson You Learned from Life?

What's the greatest lesson you've learned from life? For many, it has been said that it's simply doing the best with what they have. For others it's having the best from what they do. What you've learned from life could be a purpose, mission, or job description to leave Earth better off in some degree from how you found it.

Assuming your memoirs are about doing the best with what you have, a popular theme written about in books and media, how do you use your memoirs to stimulate your memory? The art of reminiscing is about remembering selected details of your life experiences and recording them in several ways—text, voice, video, photographs, crafts, or other memorabilia.

If you're working with those with dementia or Alzheimer's, helpful tips may be found at the Alzheimer's Foundation Web site at: help.alzfdn.org. If you're an ordinary person of any age or an educator or activities director, the gateway to writing memoirs in a variety of ways are found in creative writing classes, clubs, and groups found in nontraditional settings.

Memoirs may be put in a time capsule or gift box, transcribed from tape or digital recordings and saved on vellum or other acid-free paper. Caregivers may participate with individuals or in groups by encouraging people to talk about specific events, rites of passage, or noteworthy years. Memoirs writing may come from teenagers or older adults, parents, or anyone of any age or situation.

Or memory enhancement through memoirs writing may be intergenerational where people at different stages of life interview one another to record life story highlights, write skits or plays, or work on monologues or text and transcribe any material that's recorded, put into a computer, and saved on a DVD always with a text transcription. It's about oral history and personal history individualized.

Sound technology (not subliminal messages) using music that scientifically has shown healing results in the background may be able to help you relax as you write, speak, or illustrate your memoirs—selected significant events of your life as you reminisce. What you're aiming for as you write excerpts from your life story against a background of 'healing' music are the following results:

- Deep stress release and relaxation

- Increasing the ability to learn new tasks

- Enhanced creativity

- More focus and concentration

- Enhanced memory

- Increased feelings of well-being

Talk to music therapists about what specific healing music sounds are beneficial to learning and building new dendrites or connectors in your brain to use as your write your memoirs. Then buy a few CDs and play them softly in the background as you sit down to write, speak into a digital recorder, or illustrate.

Your first step is to do your own research on what enhances the memory. To begin, read scientific articles about the work of Thomas Budzynski, Ph.D. - University of Washington or read about the work of Dr. Fred Boersma. You may be interested in reading articles such as, "The Effect of the Relaxodont Brain Wave Synchronizer on Endodontic Anxiety.

See some of the healing music Web sites such as Jonathan Goldman's Healing Sounds Web site at: http://www.healingsounds.com/. Music is widely used for stress management and even during surgery. One of the numerous reasons for using healing sounds or music in the background when you write memoirs to invigorate your memory. The soothing music helps to create pleasant associations and cheerful memories. Examples would be sounds of the seashore, forest, or a rainy day. Combine that with aromatherapy—mild scents such as vanilla—in the background, and you have access to most of your senses.

Now add touch and texture by petting your dog or an object of memorabilia such as a photo, sculpture, stuffed toy, or fabric, and you have the stage set to freshen your memories and write, speak, or design a significant event. Learn about the power of music composed to support healing. The music you want in the background when you write your memoirs would be slow, relaxing, and have a regular beat.

There's a field of research that studies music with the tempo of healthy resting heartbeat and whether certain styles of music may synchronize your own breathing and heartbeat to it thereby slowing down your racing body rhythms. Check out some of the research to see what applies and what has worked with which category of listeners.

You want to feel relaxed and pleasant as you recall memories and write your memoirs in parts. Write for only ten minutes at a time. Then take a break and move around, exercise, or simply walk.

Check out the Light Sound Machines at Mind Machines.com. The Web site is at: http://www.mindmachines.com/. Read for yourself and decide what works best for your particular needs in stimulating your memory.

Many people enjoy relaxing, healing music in the background found on a variety of CDs. Others prefer and light and music experiences for relaxation, mild exercise or meditation. But all you really need is a pen and paper or a computer with some regular letter-writing software, such as Microsoft Word or WordPad.

Patients under anesthesia may not hear or remember the music, but their bodies hear it. You can read articles that mention how sometimes pulses adjust to the beat of the music being played. Surgeons may listen to music when operating. Not only at an unconscious level may the body rhythms synchronize to some degree with the beat of the music, but music has the power to help the surgeons focus and concentrate on doing their operations. That's why healing music is helpful in the background while you write your memoirs.

Of course you can write your memoirs without buying brain-enhancing machines, or downloading light and sound coloring books. Get started now by writing your life story—one small part at a time.

Start by writing a brief, 375 word newspaper column-style 'feature' 'anecdote' or 'article.' An anecdote is a brief reminiscence. Save it in case you want to write your memoirs as a package consisting of a dozen newspaper or magazine columns or fillers in the 250-375 range for each column.

Look at a series of weekly newspaper or magazine columns or fillers. Count the words. You'll see the preferred length for a particular publication. Notice that most columns run anywhere from 250 to 375 words—about one page of double-spaced typed material that looks similar to a news release. A press release or news release is about a page to a page and a half that usually is sent to the media with summary information about a person's achievements. News releases are announcements sent to the press about recent news or announcing a new book, product, service, or someone's accomplishments.

Next, expand your life experiences to 750 words for the magazine market. Add more material on significant events or turning points. The 750-word article now approaches the size of a brief magazine article. Or broken into two anecdotes, you have two 375-word newspaper or magazine columns or fillers. This is how you design a salable life story excerpt, write your memoirs, or recount an experience publicly. You're creating social history as living reality. Your work can become a personal essay or an anecdote about a particular time in history or an event.

Put two 750-word articles together and you now have a 1,500-word vignette that also can be used as a chapter in a book or a stand-alone magazine article of feature length.

What Other Activities Can You Combine With Writing Memoirs?

Search online or in local university libraries and read articles by the anti-aging scientist, Dr. Vincent Giampapa, a founder of the *American Academy of Anti-Aging Medicine* (A4M) and the first President of the American Board of Anti-Aging Medicine. Start at the Web site at: www.giampapainstitute.com/.

You also can read about various types of aerobics for the brain. Walking in a mall also is good activity for exercise. So is Qi Gong and Tai Chi for regaining balance in older adults.

Read about Holosync audio technology, and articles researching the work at Mt. Sinai Medical Centre. Research of Nobel Prize winner, Ilya Prigogine. Read about the work on brain and/or memory enhancement at research centers such as the Menninger Clinic, Centerpointe Research Institute, and most recently at Longevity Institute International. All these suggestions on the "use it or lose it" or investigations of what supplements work or not combined with writing your memoirs keep you busy look at new and different points of view or research.

Before you write your memoirs, you might want to read about how Holosync technology stimulates the mind, precisely creating different combinations of alpha, theta, and delta brain wave patterns. Or if you skip all this sound and light brain research information, simply sit down and write what you think are the most significant turning points, events, or experiences of your life story, writing at first in short, 350 word, then 750 word, and finally 1,500 word vignettes.

 You can flesh out or expand your anecdotes to become vignettes or pare them down to bare bones to become brief columns for the media. Whatever you write eventually can become an entire book or remain an essay or feature article. Or your columns can evolve into a play, skit, monologue, or dialogue. Another alternative is recording significant highlights of your life story as a video production of oral history and saved to a DVD as well as transcribed as text on vellum or other acid-free paper. A brief anecdote of one page may be enlarged and framed as a work of art. Or your memoirs can go into a time capsule with copies going to relatives and friends as part of your celebration of life event.

What is Reminiscence Therapy?

Gerontology classes offer courses in reminiscence therapy whereby students visit skilled nursing homes or senior assisted living apartment complexes and talk with people about their life stories, sometimes recording what they say. Reminiscence therapy is a branch of oral history and personal history, often transcribed as text and stored along with the original audio or video format in archives at oral history libraries in university libraries, such as the oral history library at University of California, Berkeley, CA.

Volunteers often record the life story highlights of veterans regarding what they saw in various wars of the past. Often recordings of military histories are donated to museums interested in what veterans saw or experienced during their wartime service.

Reminiscence therapy is being studied as to its effects on memory. The more you talk about your life experiences, the better you can remember the facts and record them to time capsules as text and multimedia.

The purpose of recording life histories to stimulate memories is to have the details in text on acid-free paper such as vellum and also to have them in multimedia format that can be transferred from one technology to another such as tape to DVD to computers and to what the next technology wave of recording will bring. There are several ways a verbal-type of person can stimulate memory—by talking and writing, creating board games and time capsules, or by recording with a camcorder and saving the video clips to a computer.

There are three primary ways to enhance or stimulate your memory by writing memoirs. You recall experiences that are positive and write or record them as writing or speaking are healing tools when used to reminisce.

You listen to background music known to enhance memory. You eat brain-nourishing foods and take food supplements customized or tailored to your body—genetically and metabolically, and exercise by walking or similar activities to get your circulation moving in a way that is conducive to better health.

Here is how to excerpt or highlight your memoirs—life story clips—and use the information to stimulate your memory. The more salable you make your life story, the more exercise you will be doing with your brain to recall. Finally, you write a eulogy about yourself in a celebration of life, while you're still alive.

Celebrate the preciousness of your consciousness while you engage in a dialogue of detail and history with your conscience. While you're doing all this, put on some healing music in the background that helps you focus and relax while you think and analyze.

Now that you've made your own bed, built your own home, it's time to build your own dendrites—the branches that connect one part of your brain to another and to the rest of you. Writing memoirs to help your memory is about putting direct experience in a small package and launching it in a time capsule that you review periodically and add to.

Write Tributes, Eulogies, and Celebration of Life Templates

As a celebration of life, write highlights of your life story while you're are still able to. Here's what to ask before you write a eulogy of yourself or anyone else for a celebration of life party:

1. With what kind of activities are you involved?

2. Do research online to find out the exact information about a particular activity in which you participated (or ask the same for someone about whom you're writing this eulogy).

3. Track down someone who can give you information about some project you worked with—such as a scholarship fund or volunteer work. You'll have to make several phone calls to get names of people to talk to.

4. Check out and get approval from anyone you talked with to include this type of information in your celebration of life eulogy. If you're going to publish your memoirs as a salable life story excerpt, this step is important. You can write a eulogy in text format. Or it can become a video or audio clip to go into a time capsule or gift box of memories.

Tribute or Eulogy Template

Here is a template you can use for writing eulogies. Just fill in the blanks with your own information. A eulogy can be a celebration of life time capsule. Or it can be created for someone who is no longer here.

Tribute or Eulogy for Celebration of Life Ceremony

To (insert the name of a publication you're sending this to if this is for the public). For more information, contact: (insert your name and phone number as well as email address)

Your name or name of person about whom you're writing the eulogy, age, city, date, announcement in one paragraph made up of two sentences. Wife/husband of (insert number of years). Wife/husband's occupation, the status of the person now. If living, announcement of a celebration of life ceremony or party. If not living, how the person passed on. Mention the spouse, if any, and number of years married. Insert where the person lives or lived, since what year. Mention how many children and their names, and where the children graduated from, if relevant.

Insert what you enjoy or have enjoyed for years. Put in an experience that you feel is most important such as "person and spouse bought a house in _____ in (insert year), although, (name of city) remained their home. Insert any accomplishment such as "in (month, year) insert name of person accomplished this (such as placed second in the _____ _______ race at (insert town) and was awarded a ______(insert what award was given).

After (insert person's name) retired from (name of company and what the company does), which (name of person founded, if relevant), his/her son/daughter took over the business. (Insert anything relevant to the person's life story in one sentence.)

Put here any survivors such as " Besides his/her husband/wife and children, he/she is survived by his/her sister, ABC, his son's wife, XYZ, and two grandchildren: (insert names of grandchildren) example: 123 and 456.

 Now finish with what schools you or whomever you're writing the eulogy about attended, such as "A graduate of XYZ High School in (city) and of the (ABC College of state), name of person is/ (insert main accomplishment in life) example: _____ was a pioneer in the launching and support of a project that encourages high-achieving XYZ graduates to attend ABC College. The program pays full tuition and gives each student a laptop computer, a monthly stipend, and free admission to cultural institutions in (insert name of state). Since the program's inception in (year), (insert number of) students have been enrolled in the program.

If the person you're writing the eulogy about is no longer living, you may add a paragraph that says something like "Contributions in memory of (insert name of person) may be made to ABC College Fund/ (name of fund) and sent to (insert name), Project Director, ABC Scholarship Program, (insert street address, city, state, zip code, Web site, email address).

If your eulogy is about a living person celebrating a Celebration of Life ceremony, you can substitute "Contributions to raise funds for (name of person's) favorite charity may be made to (insert name and address of the project director). A eulogy can be something you experience while living as a celebration of your own memoirs as a project for memory enhancing and reminiscing.

How Reminiscence as an Activity is used to Stimulate Memory

An activity called reminiscence involves recalling details of your life that happened in the past. It's personal history. Behavioral, counseling, activities, and health professionals sometimes use life story reminiscing in a group to encourage interpersonal skills. Memoirs writing, speaking, or designing lets you dialogue with yourself, with empty chairs and yourself, or with a group of people or one other person.

Exchanging excerpts, highlights, and turning points of life stories means focusing on significant events. It's also a way to share values, commitment, and skills. Memoirs writing is an act of teaching—either yourself or another. You can have closure or more power over your decisions. The goal of finding peace and serenity from memoirs writing may also bring up memories that you'd rather forget.

Every life is important and worth a book, play, skit, or vignette. When healthcare professionals use reminiscence therapy they are using writing as a healing tool. For those who are not so verbal, memorabilia, photos, illustrations, talking, crafts, or objects contribute to recorded and transcribed memoirs. The outcome from memoirs is that a story comes seemingly from nothing and a script develops.

Writing memoirs is one way to relieve stress, especially during times of grieving or seeking closure. When you tell or write your memoirs, your self-esteem, image, and inner core are made public (only to you and/or to others). Your goal is intimacy.

You are seeing into yourself. You are sharing meaning with yourself and, if desired, with others. If you decide to share your memoirs, it's another form of communication since communication is defined as sharing meaning.

For those who don't enjoy writing about themselves, music can elicit memories of events in your life that happened when you first heard the music or from the way the music makes you feel or move. You can take a photo or paint a picture or look at memorabilia and ephemera (such as postcards you saved or letters sent to you many years ago).

Other ways of bringing back memories is through touching various textures, smelling different foods and spices, such as ethnic dishes your relatives or friends may have served you on certain holidays or during certain events. You can look at wedding memorabilia, children's pictures, or yourself when very young.

School yearbooks and photos also help bring back memories. Memories can come back from touching textures, such as the feel of a dog's fur, a special dish, or a prayer scroll.

Use scents such as jasmine and orange blossom water to evoke memories of certain places or times. The idea is to use all your senses and then write, speak, or design the memory that pops into your head.

The whole idea of writing your memoirs is to use the past to make the present a better place.

It's an informative act, not a directive act. You're informing, not directing. You can use memories to review your life.

Mental health professionals call this act "life review." The purpose of reviewing your life is to find closure.

You also can use writing memoirs to solve a problem, get results, or dissolve conflicts. If you've had a tough life, memories can be stressful rather than pleasant and relaxing. You could flash back to an incident where someone treated you harshly.

You've got to put your foot down and say 'stop' to yourself and think of something pleasant— such as switching to a scene of tall pine trees in nature, parks, or mountain views.

At least you find the chance to face the issues and resolve them by reaching closure either by dialoguing with an empty chair to represent the person you want to address, or writing or speaking your mind to accept the closure. Whichever path you choose to remember, it's all about putting direct experience in a small package by starting with a brief column or vignette.

You can keep it private or write salable memoirs and launch your memories world-wide. If you launch publicly, be sure to have foot notes in your memoirs to back up your statements with the resources for your facts, when available. Here's how to start.

Put Direct Experience In A Small Package And Launch It Worldwide.

Here's How to Write, Edit, Dramatize, Package, Promote, Present, Publish & Launch Personal Histories, Autobiographies, Biographies, Vignettes, and Eulogies: Launching the Inspiration-Driven or Design-Driven Life Story and Detailing Your Purpose.

How to Write Personal History Essays: Text or Video

Use personal or biographical experiences as examples when you write your vignette, column, skit, play, life story, or essay. Begin by using specific examples taken from your personal experience, personal history, or biographical resources.

Start with a general statement. Then relate the general to your specific personal experience. You don't have to only write about yourself. You can write about someone else as long as you have accurate historical facts about that person, and you state your credible resources.

Here's an example of two opening sentences that state the general and then give the specific personal experience. "Mom's a space garbage woman. She repairs satellites."

Let's analyze all the different parts of an informed argument essay. By analyzing the result in depth instead of only skimming for breadth, you will be able to write concretely from different points of view.

You'll learn how to construct an essay from bare bones--from its concept. You start with a concept. Then you add at least three specific examples to your concept until it develops into a mold. A mold is a form, skeleton or foundation. Think of concept as conception. Think of mold as form or skeleton. Think of awning as the outer skin that covers the whole essay and animates it into lively writing.

You don't want your essay to be flat writing. You want writing that is animated, alive, and able to move, motivate, or inspire readers. Finally, you cover the mold with an awning.

The mold is your pit, skeleton or foundation. Your mold contains your insight, foresight, and hindsight. It has the pitfalls to avoid and the highlights. You need to put flesh on its bones.

Then you need to cover your mold with an awning.

You need to include or protect that concept and mold or form by including it under this awning of a larger topic or category. The awning holds everything together. It's your category under which all your related topics fall. That's what the technique of organizing your essay or personal history is all about.

In other words, concept equals form plus details. *Story equals concept plus details.* That's the math formula for writing an essay if you'd like to put it into a logical equation of critical thinking. C = Fo + De. Or S = C + De. That's what you need to remember about writing an essay. Your concept is composed of your *form* (mold, *foundation*, or skeleton) and *details*. A concept isn't an idea. It's the *application* of your idea.

A concept is what your story is about. Your concept is imbedded in your story. A story can mean your *personal history* or any other story or anecdote in your essay, or any *highlight* of your life or specific life experience. A concept also can be a *turning point* such as *rites of passage* or take place at *any* stage of life.

Your story fleshes out your concept as you add more and more details. To create a story you take your concept which is your form plus details. Then you add more and more details to your original concept to move the plot forward and flesh out your story.

The characters drive the action forward. That's how memoirs become salable books that move the action or experiences faster and faster as page turners and at the end either solve a problem or show what you learned from your mistakes or choices. The conclusion answers the question: What's the most important lesson you have learned from life?

One typical answer would be "I learned to make the most of what I have." Then you fill in the details using vivid, colorful, specific, concrete examples. You're writing an adventure not a laundry list of facts.

When writing about events in your life as an informed argument, you will be able to give examples backed up with resources. That's what makes a memoirs essay great--knowing what examples to put into the essay at which specific points in time.

Gone will be general, vague, or sweeping statements. Therefore, I'd like each of you on this learning team to start planning your essay by analyzing and discussing the parts that chronologically go into the essay. That's how you organize essays in a linear fashion.

Take an essay apart just as you would take a clock or computer apart, and put it back together. Now all the parts fit and work. Taking apart an essay helps you understand how to plan and write your own essay-writing assignments or personal history as a time capsule.

Here's how to take a memoirs essay apart. To analyze an essay in depth, you break the essay down into its six parts: statement-of-position, description, argumentation, exposition, supplementation and evaluation. These parts of an essay also are explained in the book titled, *The Informed Argument*. (ISBN: 0155414593). For more ideas, you also can look at some action verbs in another book titled, *801 Action Verbs for Communicators*. (ISBN: 0-595-31911-4).

Before you even get to the expressive part of life story-related argumentation, you have to state your position and describe it by using specific examples. Then you get to the informed argument in the middle of your essay. After you've finished arguing logically using critical thinking and your resources, you use exposition.

Then you use supplementation, and finally evaluation.

To practice writing personal history essays in text or on video, define and analyze the words 'exposition' and 'supplementation.' Use exposition and supplementation in at least one sentence each as an example of how you would use it in your essay. Don't stick to only what is familiar.

My dictionary defines 'exposition' as "a careful setting out of the facts or ideas involved in something." The principal themes are presented first in a 'music' exposition. Apply it now to an essay. Present your principal themes first in your personal history. Supplementation means adding to your work to improve or complete it.

The goal of a memoirs essay is to analyze your informed argument in depth. That's why there are six parts to an essay. Knowing what those six parts are as well as showing examples that give you the experience you need to plan and organize your essay. A memoirs essay focuses on telling publicly your point of view as a persuasive argument using critical thinking. It's different from the diary-first-person memoirs that illustrates your point of view metaphorically.

The result of using an argument to persuade in a memoirs essay is that once you have organized your plan in writing, the life experience details essay almost writes itself. Keep an old saying, proverb, slogan, or motto in front of you when you write to remind you of the closure you want or the conclusion that you want to emphasize as you persuade your readers.

You don't have to defend your point of view when you have the details factually represented by evidence such as credible resources that can be fact-checked by readers. You may want to show evidence, credibility, or that some other research is flawed or not flawed. In a persuasive memoirs essay, your argument is a tool used to persuade and convince. Your goal is to be reassuring about certain events in your life story.

A salable magazine filler also can be an anecdote sent to a magazine. The anecdote may be expanded into a column or news release and then into a salable vignette. A feature can be fleshed out into a book chapter, and finally into a skit, play, true story, article, or memoirs book, or presented as a novel, biography, or autobiography. It's a matter of linking the columns or anecdotes you write into articles and stories that each have a beginning, middle, and end.

Consider also the online opportunities from audio or video podcasts to blogs (web logs) and e-zines. Content online or on discs is in demand when it serves a purpose and has a specific attitude. Use fresh angles on new trends or unfamiliar details. Look for patterns in your life story and connect the links.

\#

Here Are 50 Strategies on How to Write Your Life Story or Anyone Else's:

Start with a Vignette or Column….Link the Vignettes…Dramatize….and Novelize.

1.   Contact anyone's family members to gain permission to write their family member's memorials.

2.   Write memoirs of various clerical or other religious or social leaders.

3.   Write two to four dozen memorials for houses of worship. Put these memorials in a larger book of memoirs for various organizations, religious groups, houses of worship, or professional associations.

4.	Find a model for your biographies.

5.	These could be based on a book of vocational biographies or centered on any other aspect of life such as religious or community service as well as vocations.

6.	Read the various awards biographies written and presented for well-known people.

7.	Focus on the accomplishments that stand out of these people or of you if you're writing an autobiography.

8.	Use oral eulogies as your foundation. You'll find many oral eulogies that were used in memorial services.

9.	Consult professionals who conduct memorial services to look at their eulogies written for a variety of people and presented at memorial services.

10.	Stick to the length of a eulogy. You'll find the average eulogy runs about 1,500 to 1,800 words. That' is what's known as magazine article average length. Most magazines ask for feature articles of about 1,500 words. So your eulogies should run that same length.

11.	When read aloud, they make up the eulogy part of a memorial service. At 250 to 300 words double-spaced per page, it comes to about five-to-seven pages and is read aloud in about seven to 10 minutes.

12.   Take each 1,500-1,800 word eulogy and focus on the highlights, significant events, and turning points. Cut the eulogy down to one page of printed magazine-style format.

13.   Keep the eulogy typeset so that it all fits on one page of printed material in 12 point font.

14.   You can package one-page eulogies for memorial services or include a small photo on the page if space permits.

15.   Cut the eulogy down to 50-70 words, average 60 words for an oral presentation using PowerPoint software for a computer-based slide show complete with photos.

16.   Put the PowerPoint show on a CD or DVD. Use the shorter eulogy focusing on significant points in the person's life. The purpose of a PowerPoint eulogy is to show the person lived a purposeful life—a design-driven, goal-driven life with purpose and concrete meaning in relation to others.

17.   Write biographies, memoirs, and autobiographies by focusing on the highlights of someone's life or your own life story. Turn

personal histories into life stories that you can launch in the media. You need to make a life story salable. It is already valuable.

18.   Read autobiographies in print. Compare the autobiographies written by ghostwriters to those written by the authors of autobiographies who write about their own experiences.

19.   Read biographies and compare them to autobiographies written by ghost writers and those written as diary novels in first person or as genre novels in first person. Biographies are written in third person.

20.   If you write a biography in third person keep objective. If you write an autobiography in first person you can be subjective or objective if you bring in other characters and present all sides of the story equally.

21.   If you're writing a biography, whose memories are you using? If you write an autobiography, you can rely on your own memory. Writing in the third person means research verifying facts and fact-checking your resources for credibility. How reliable is the information?

22.   Use oral history transcriptions, personal history, videos, audio tapes, and interviews for a biography. You can use the same for an

autobiography by checking for all sides of the story with people involved in the life story— either biography or autobiography.

23.   With personal histories and oral histories, be sure to obtain letters of permission and to note what is authorized. Celebrities in the public eye are written about with unauthorized or authorized biographies. However, people in private life who are not celebrities may not want their name or photo in anyone's book. Make sure everything you have is in writing in regard to permissions and what information is permitted to be put into your book or article, especially working with people who are not celebrities and those who are.

24.   When interviewing, get written approval of what was said on tape. Let the person see the questions beforehand to be able to have time to recall an answer with accuracy regarding facts and dates or times of various events. Give peoples' memories a chance to recall memories before the interview.

25.   Write autobiographies in the first person in genre or diary format. You can also dramatize the autobiography in a play or skit first and then flesh it out into novel format. Another alternative is to focus only on the

highlights, events, and turning points in various stages of life.

26.   Ghost-written autobiographies usually are written in the first person. A ghost-writer may have a byline such as "as told to" or "with____(name of ghostwriter)."

27.   Condense experience in small chunks or paragraphs. Use the time-capsule approach. Use vignettes. Focus on how people solved problems or obtained results or reached a goal. Find out whether the person wants you to mention a life purpose. Emphasize how the person overcame challenges or obstacles.

28.   In an autobiography, instead of dumping your pain on others because it may be therapeutic for you, try to be objective and focus on what you learned from your choices and decisions and how what you learned transformed your life. Be inspirational and nurturing to the reader. Tell how you learned, what you learned, how you rose above your problems, and how you transcended the trouble. Focus on commitment and your relationship to others and what your purpose is in writing the autobiography.

29.   Stay objective. Focus on turning points, highlights, and significant events and their

relationship to how you learned from your mistakes or choices and rose above the trouble. Decide what your life purpose is and what points you want to emphasize. If you want to hide facts, decide why and what good it will do the reader. Stay away from angry writing and focus instead on depth and analysis.

30.	Don't use humor if it puts someone down, including you. Don't put someone down to pick yourself up.

31.	Make sure your writing doesn't sound like self-worship or ego soothing. Don't be modest, but don't shock readers either.

32.	Before you write your salable autobiography, find out where the market is and who will buy it. If there is no market, use print-on-demand publishing and select a title most likely to be commercial or help market your book. At least you can give copies to friends and family members. Or self-publish with a printer. Another way to go is to self-publish using print-on-demand software yourself. Then distribute via advertising or the Internet and your Web site.

33.	You'd be surprised at how many people would be interested in your life story if it were packaged, designed, and promoted. So launch your life story in the media before you publish. Write your life story as a novel or play or both. Every life story has value. I believe all life stories are salable. The hard part is finding the correct niche market for your experiences. So focus on what you are and what you did so people with similar interests, hobbies, or occupations may learn from you. Market to people who are in the same situation as you are.

34.   Divide your biography into the 12 stages of life. Then pare down those 12 significant events or turning points and rites of passage into four quarters—age birth to 25 (young adult), age 26-50 (mature adult), age 51-75 (creative adult) and age 76-100 (golden years of self fulfillment).

35.   Start with a vignette focusing on each of the most important events and turning points of your life. Do the same in a biography, only writing in third person. For your own life story, write in first person.

36.   What's important for the reader to know about your life in relation to social history and the dates in time? For example, what did you do during the various wars?

37.   Keep a journal or diary, and record events as they happen. Focus on how you relate

to social history. Write in your diary each day. Use the Web and create a diary or Web blog.

38.   If you keep a daily journal, and make sure it is saved on a computer disk or similar electronic diary, you can put the whole journal together and create a book or play online or have a digital recording of your life. It's your time capsule in virtual reality.

39.   A daily journal will keep memories fresh in your mind when you cut down to significant events for a book. You want to recall significant events in detail with resources.

40.   If you're young, keep a daily journal on a computer disk and keep transferring it from one technology to the next as technology evolves. Keep a spare saved and up on the Web so you can download it anytime. Use some of the free Web site space available to people online.

41.   If you write a book when you're older, at least you'll have all the youthful memories in detail where you can transfer the notes from one computer to another or upload from your disk to a browser for publication with a print-on-demand publisher.

42.   Keep writing short vignettes. Include all the details as soon as possible after the event

occurs. When you are ready to write a book, you'll be able to look back rationally and from a much more objective and mature perspective on the details. Then you can decide what to put into a salable life story that's about to be published.

43.   Don't listen to people who tell you that if you are not famous, your life story is only fit for your own family because no one else will buy it. Fiddle-de-sticks!

44.   There are events that happened to you or experiences in your line of work, travel, parenting, research, or lifestyle that people want to read because you have experiences to share.

45.   Find a niche market of people with similar interests and market your life story to them.

46.   Try out the waters first with a short vignette in magazines. If the magazines buy your vignette, your slice of life story, then you can write a book. Can you imagine if all the travelers and archaeologists, parenting experts and teachers didn't value their life story to the point that they thought it was fit only for relatives (who may be the only ones not interested in reading it because they already

know your life story). In fact, your relatives may be angry at you for spilling the details to the public.

47.   Instead, focus on that part of your life where you made a choice or decision with which everyone can identify. Inspire and motivate readers. If your experience is universal, we can all identify with it. We all go through the same stages of life.

48.   So let us know how you overcame your obstacles, solved problems, and rose above the keen competition.

49.   Or if you didn't, let us know how you learned to live with and enjoy your life. Readers want nourishment. If your life isn't about making a difference in the world, then write about how you handled what we all go through.

50.   We want to read about the joy of life, and your design-driven life full of purpose, meaning, and inspiration. We want to read about the universal in you with which we can identify. Most of all readers want information in a life story or personal history from which we can make our own choices. Keep your life story as a novel to 12 to 24 short chapters. Write in short, readable chunks.

#

Chapter Two:

Writing Your Life Story or a Biography as a Play or Skit before You Write it as a Novel

Intergenerational Writing as Commitment to Values

Adolescents write life story excerpts of significant events and turning points—as they enter their senior year of secondary school. Here are their monologues or essays of intergenerational values. Their purpose is to inform the reader by using excerpts of life story highlights, significant events, and turning points.

Below are three written life story excerpts in essay format submitted to me by three young women that are students at Islamic High Schools in the U.S.A. These slice-of-life memoirs as essays were chosen because they represent specific highlights in the lives of the young women who wished to remain anonymous.

The life story essays emphasize some of the adolescents' values. They present an intergenerational voice. The writing presented by youth to those over age 65 makes the effort in writing intergenerational as a response to senior citizens who write their life stories for adolescent readers.

The writing of the adolescents gives resilience to the voice of youth. It is a voice of self-esteem and confidence within the rigorous academic program they study to prepare for university work and graduate study beyond. The students take four years of college-preparatory math, science, English, other languages, history, and religion plus advanced placement tests in science and math. Males and females attend separate classes.

The monologues or essays were emailed to a fellow student who then emailed the essays to me with information removed as to their names, cities, or schools. They are examples of what several female high-school students wanted to write about: what it is like to attend an Islamic High School in the USA. The writing gives the self-confident young women a buoyant voice, not a voice of resignation, in planning their futures. They express their values in their own voices.

Title: Why Is It All Normal?

Essay #1 – Age 16 Female- Private Islamic High School, USA Eastern Coast States

Life can't be described in one word. It can't be described in more than one word. There aren't enough words in any language. Knowledge isn't even a sea, or so I've heard. It's actually in reality, an expanding universe.

I learn so much, waking up and breathing every day, almost routine, but I still learn so much. Life isn't so robotic, and redundant, unless you make it that way. You never learn from your mistakes, or the mistakes of others. That's just it right there, you can never put rules on how life runs itself, because there are rules for certain things, and for others it's just life. I realized so many new things about my life. I'll never get to a point of 'saturation,' 'satisfaction,' or 'idleness."

I've felt so many new emotions and discovered new things about human nature. I write to my friend, e-mailing her the details of my accounts and anecdotes. Therefore I should have retained some accounts that I should relate to give a clear enough portrayal to prove my point.

I really try to share all that I learn, but sometimes it's difficult to communicate. I also should remember because I love to preserve a memory, which is why I photograph any occasion that I can. I would want to replay those memories again and again, to try to relive them. Sadly all the reminiscing can result in time consumption without result or gain.

It's not about self-gain. Equate success to how much 'memory' left behind, what you've done for others, nothing more. We are subject to mortal limitations. The evanescence lies in everything, don't deny it. I've been told to record my thoughts.

I've always seen written thoughts as "dangerous" but now, there are certain thoughts that are perilous, due to the boundaries of our complexities.

Every year I grow, and I think the middle teenage years are that of maturity like no other. Don't waste time, please. Ironically I feel that I could be wasting yours. Without any more of this vagueness, I will commence relating accounts you should find interest in.

You never thought that school could ever be fun, or life-altering. It was always so boring and routine. It was just something that you had to do, it was the only thing that you could do, so it was a time-consumer, that's all.

As a child, I didn't want to go to college. I didn't even think that I'd get to high school-not my grades; it just felt really far away (in time). School was always so far from what I wished it could be. I didn't like it that much.

My friends would come and go, and they still do to this day. Some leave because they didn't have enough money, some for their parents' jobs, some I'll never know. Others just grew apart from me.

I basically never actually had real friends. (Just one, but I only realized this about a year ago, or a year and a half ago.) It was a friendship that was said, not actually meant.

I tried. I really tried to make more friends or be friends when I said I was. I'm the kind who doesn't like to lie, especially to myself. I don't like illusions.

I don't like the fact that people like to live in dreams. And just because I have guts to say "What's the point? We're going to die anyway." People say I'm too pessimistic. I like to think I'm more of a realist. I view things from a bigger outlook. I don't see life's events as a teenage drama. It's really simulated.

Teenagers are stupid, they make life the way they think it might be, and they dramatize everything. Matters are fine and teenagers make it seem like the world is falling out of orbit. Most are stable, and out of peer pressure (what a surprise, they create it), they lose control. It's completely pointless.

They force themselves to pretend to like the latest trends, or pretend to enjoy the new movies. I realized, I could do it, but like I said, I don't lie to myself. So I catch myself before I fall. I try to clear it up, and sometimes it doesn't work.

At parties, I dance with my friends, and I notice how others get attention, because they dance well, because they're creative, or they can bend in more than one way. Then I realize, wait, that's not a priority. I'm just supposed to have fun, and my dancing doesn't need to be like theirs', otherwise, it wouldn't be my style. Also, with trends, like the ripped jeans, I never bothered buying a pair. It's expensive and useless, clothes are supposed to cover.

Cell phones

Do they have to have a camera, and mobile web, and those features that companies overcharge you for? Along with the 300 dollar phone, you get a plan that causes your bill to skyrocket. It's bad enough we have to pay for gas that's completely necessary, and completely draining us. Ask yourself, why in the world do you have aim on your phone? You don't use it. Text messages I use, rather than calling, and talking on the phone, send a quick text. Did you buy a Razr too? If you did, it's a lucky guess.

Then again, people are experiencing a superficial prosperity, like the 1920s in America. How many credit cards do you have, how many "debt solution" companies are there?

Does it all make sense now? I hope it does. Read "The Great Gatsby," by F. Scott Fitzgerald. I did. Whoever knew I'd learn things from that? I read it late nights, with a bookmark that I sprayed with "Burberry" perfume so I wouldn't get bored. I did anyway.

I learned from it later. I like to experience, and then learn from mistakes. History repeats itself, and doesn't that mean that people never evolve? If the human race evolved, we really might be perfect beings by now, and that can't happen.

My junior year was a great experience, because the girls in my class were close to each other. There still is lack of trust, and close ties, and stuff like that. A friendship can't completely form except over time. Unfortunately, people breathe envy from their nostrils when they see us laughing and having fun together, so we pray we stay together.

I only have one real friend that has lasted for so long, she has my birthday, and she's two years younger. I don't always call her, but we're there for each other at special times, and we can call up each other like we've been together the day before. It's a beautiful thing.

She's been there since I could remember, but I have a really special friend that I met a few years ago. She's there good, and bad, and she never let go, and she's been through worse, that's even more beautiful. We talk, and laugh, and we've become one person, she holds a piece of me now. I really don't know how I could live without her. She's like my biological sister, but I'm grateful she's not. Otherwise it wouldn't be the same.

I honestly have a story to tell for each day of junior year. It's amazing. We have something called "Hobo Friday." It's when the whole 11th grade class sat outside our homeroom and ate lunch together. We usually eat in the homeroom, but there's a class in there that day and we can't sit outside because of the bugs and dirt, and heat, and snow, and the lunch room is bootlegged.

My school is small, it's one building, and the gym, and the cafeteria is one place. The gym is small, on the top floor. The classrooms are not huge. The senior class was about 30 people, and the junior class was about 31, the other classes reached about 40, 50, about that much.

The parking lot is big, and the land area around is nice, but they can't create space (lebensraum). I learned this meant living space in German in my US History class. They are not allowed. My school also is private.

So we're lacking in so much more than I hoped for. Now I block it all out, it doesn't bother me that I don't have the chance like others do, and that I don't have the best people around me. Sadly I'm used to it.

A nail pricks me every day, and I stopped crying. The mark is there, but I hide it. I appreciate what I have, and just live my life to the best ability that I can. That's what matters.

The bathrooms are on hiatus. They were painted by a few senior girls. The fountains are not drinkable. I warn people not to drink from them, and I think it's because my mom has inculcated the thought that I could get lead poisoning if I drank from the fountains.

The school has a really old heating system, and they can't fix it, it's too, obsolete. I don't feel that my teachers really cared to teach me, except a few, like my history teacher, and my physics teacher. My math teachers, and other teachers too, but I don't need to mention them all, it's useless.

They were hard, and I regret that they were. I still believe I could have learned everything they wanted me to without having to work me like a pack mule. My Arabic teacher made fun of my accent.

I speak in the Syrian Dialect, and she doesn't. She wasn't encouraging, and I didn't like that. She made me want to never learn, or speak Arabic. I do speak, my friends like the way I do, it's different, and it's ludicrous when they try to imitate me. They embarrass Syrians, and I mean that as a joke.

We make fun of each other, and we always knew what to say. For example, making fun of vices and follies are our specialties. Once I was walking out of school. My mother always reminds me to concentrate and do one thing at a time, and to keep track of my surroundings.

I try to listen, but I failed myself. My brother has a G35 Coupe Infiniti 2004, and his friend has another sports car in the same color he does, midnight blue. They both have tinted windows, and it almost looks the same-to someone who's not paying attention. I wasn't paying attention, my brother called to me, and the cars were parked near each other. I was letting my instincts lead me, and like I said, it was feeling routine.

Usually the boys are around my brother's car, and this time they weren't, they were around his friend's car. I walked into his car.

I opened his door, and almost sat in. I got knocked into reality when my brother yelled out "What the hell are you doing?!"

Then I retreated and stopped thinking about my school events, and ran away with all the boys laughing at me, I sat in my brother's car after running around yelling "Oh my God! I'm so sorry!" They all laughed, and they made fun of me a few times after that. I let it fade away. My friend told me I was so zoned out, that she was calling me at that time, and I didn't hear a thing. High school is overrated.

I talk loud sometimes, and I love to have fun, and smile and I know that I have to make the best of time, even though I don't listen to that small voice inside. Sometimes I silence it, and that's not a good thing.

I know that I'm planning things, but I don't know the details of the event. For example, I was determined to go to my appointment to take off my braces, but I didn't know it would hurt, or that I'd end up staying at the orthodontist's for about 3 hours.

Also, I was determined one day to present my movie project for my English class, but I didn't know that I'd run around looking for things, and that I would have a hard time trying to find a projector and computer hook up for my VCD (no AV club, just a Computer Lab with all the AV equipment).

I also did know that my brother was responsible for us going to school and coming home, but I didn't know that for many days of his senior year, he'd make me run around last period looking for a ride home, or tell me to go home with other people. It gave a bad impression sometimes when I came up to people, "Hey, can I have a ride home?"

I had a lot of mixed emotions recently, similar to "I love it, but I hate it." I also realized that I don't go through half the mental and psychological problems a lot of kids go through in my age. It's mainly because I don't make my life a teenage drama, it's so pointless.

I'm probably a late bloomer relative to my contemporaries, but then again, they're actually early bloomers, but sadly it's not taboo to think or discuss what they do. They think about boys, and girls, and discuss gossip, and useless time consuming topics. Their minds wander into the "Twilight Zone" and places they shouldn't be.

They ask questions that they can't answer themselves. So they confuse and torture themselves relentlessly in their minds. They ask what if this or that happened. Once during lunch, I walked away from girls in my class hoping they wouldn't realize I did, because they were discussing weird topics.

Instead they asked whether I was depressed. I'm not, I never was, and I don't plan on being that way. I spent most of my years finding myself, and keeping myself "grounded."

I don't remember being really happy in school, but rather more happy out of school. I'd laugh, but it hurt inside because it never felt like the second home it was supposed to be. I was more detached from it all. I was only attached because I had to be there. My parents couldn't think of an alternate solution. I usually put on an outside guise of "everything's peachy."

Depression

Do you know how evident and apparent it is? It's almost a plague. Zoloft, Ambien, and other sleep medications are being given out like Tylenol. "Hey you know your friend's father? Don't bother her, he has depression. And the other guy has schizophrenia." Why is it all normal?

Then again, like I always say, it's all a state of mind, love, composure, whatever you want. My friends said I sound like a hippie, as if they know the history of hippies. All they know is that hippies wear tie-dyed shirts, and have peace signs. It's all a state of mind, but I'm human. I'm never going to completely learn. I could keep writing, but I can't. I'd never finish.

It's the simple things in life, like the trips on holidays to the movies, bowling, shopping days, and parties. I don't see movies frequently.

Honestly, you always think you know what's best, what you want, what you need, but it's not true. You think you know that you need to do this or that, but you never know what's truly best for you. It's completely empty, a total void.

You think you're supposed to have fun, and go to parties (only girls), but that's materialistic, and selfish. Success is defined by you. I define it as being able to help others, and only achieve for others.

Now that high school is coming to an end, it seems so much better because I've come a long way from where I was--in a shell that I created. And now I have broken out. I've seen the surroundings, and sometimes I walk in the wrong direction but I go back, and I pick myself up and move on. Ignore me now, but never say I didn't warn you.

#

Life Lessons

Essay #2– Age 16 Female- Islamic High School, USA Eastern Coast States

Throughout life we learn many lessons. We go through a journey while facing many obstacles. While doing so, we are taught by many different people. The teachings of my parents included how to walk, talk, and always eat my vegetables, and most importantly how to treat others the way I would like to be treated.

The teachings of my younger siblings especially my eight year old brother (my only brother) included how to enjoy life and how my brother can sit down by himself and still have a good time. They taught me to smile and to appreciate everything I have. Also, my youngest sibling taught me responsibility. I was nine when he was born. I was able to watch him grow into the wonderful boy that he is right now.

While in elementary school, I had many great teachers. Some till this day I can never forget. When entering high school, I realized this is just the beginning. I entered a private school during

7th grade and had so many memories from that time. I went into 7th grade not knowing what was going to happen.

I expected to walk in and make a few friends, go through problems, have good times, bad times-- everything. However, to be quite honest, I received much more then what I expected. We started with about 24 girls and then slowly decreased. Now our class consists of 16 girls. They are the girls who went through everything with me. I love them dearly, and I'd give everything for them.

'Words,' five simple letters...yet there are not enough to express to you how I feel about my friends. Well you can call them friends. I on the other hand would much rather call them sisters.

Like one of my friends likes to say, "Not even Kodak can capture our memories." Or to quote Vitamin C "...as we go on, we remember all the times we had together, and as our lives change from whatever we will still be friends forever..."

Ten years from now I won't remember every joke that was ever told, or every "hobo Friday" that happened, but I will remember that my friends were always there, and they will continue to be there for me.

When I entered the private school that I am currently attending, I must be honest with you, the first thought that went through my mind was "Man, I can't wait to get out of here," but as my senior year slowly approaches, I start to think of how could I have been so naïve.

Little did I know that this school would become more of a second home. I will definitely miss high school, and it's where I met my friends. That's where I learned the quadratic equations and probability (which can actually help you in life believe it or not) thanks to my math teacher or shall I say teachers.

It's where I learned the history of our country and even though some might think, "Oh, who cares about the history; all that matters is what we are now," believe it or not, history does repeat itself, and your history helps build up your future.

High school is not only where I learned about Shakespeare in English class, or about the environment during science period. I learned many other lessons.

I learned that the world is full of choices, and once we step outside we venture into a world full of possibilities. The most important lesson that I learned would have to be that everything happens for a reason. Think about it. If what happened yesterday or a month didn't actually happen, would you be where you are right now?

#

A Long-Term Decision

Essay #3 – Age 16 Female- Islamic High School, USA Eastern Coast States

Sometimes looking back you regret your decisions, but you console yourself by saying it's what God wanted. I guess that's how it started for me when I decided to go to my Islamic school and give up the Americanized dream school in Egypt. However, as you grow older, you tend to see the bigger picture, why you were really put in that position.

 In the beginning, my new school was not exactly a dream come true. The class consisted of about 20 girls that were all really nice but I still missed my old school. The work load was a slap in the face. I was accustomed to reading two novels a year, and my new teacher walked in first day telling us we would read up to 9 or 10.

Obviously, I was the only one in shock. I quickly learned the school rules, much different than the ones in my old school but being the good girl that I am, I complied with every one of them.

 Now that I am a junior, and after the passing of five years, it scares me to think that one day I will graduate and leave my new school. As the vice principal put it, we are protected within the school's "golden gates".

Not to say that we are not social or can not face society, but we have simply become a family, not just friends. You walk into a school of about 260 students and 25 staff members. As the years go by, the kids in your grade and younger and older ones become friends, sisters, brothers. And the staff, well they become your guardians, always watching out for you. I do not wish to make it sound like a utopian society, because it is plagued like any other school with gossip, stink bombs, suspension warnings.....the whole nine yards.

#

Suspension and Expulsion:

Being in a strict school where all the students are going to go to college if it is the last thing the staff does, you are likely to hear the words expulsion and suspension no less than twice a day. Be it in a threatening tone or a hidden one:

"Good morning student, your shoe laces are suspended...I mean untied." It has gotten to a point where we no longer care.

The staff knows it and every now and then will suspend a person to remind us...no one is safe. On Sports Day we decided as a junior class to ditch and go to IHOP. Let me tell you when we got back we were in a lot of trouble. We thought the administration was going to pass out suspension warnings like candy.

Again as a class we decided to go apologize (after we got yelled at of course). When we went to apologize the vice principal told us that we were the school's responsibility, and she said that she would forget the whole incident because she has children too, and she knows kids will be kids.

I love how the staff, especially my physics teacher always tells us that we are like her children. Guess that's what they mean by the "golden gates." But we will never stop testing the waters. Maybe it's our extra sense of taking advantage of being protected...at least for now.

Teenage Pressures

 Our principal always talks to us. I do not know if he thinks we do not listen and still talks or if he is really convinced that we are listening.

Most of the time we aren't, but once in a blue moon we do listen to him. Smoking, drinking and drugs are not even approached issues, because we are really good kids. We know that in Islam anything that harms your health is prohibited, and I am glad we know that and are convinced, be it a 7th grader or a senior.

One day, when I was actually listening, or I snapped out of a day dream, I am not sure, I heard him say that the teenage years are not as hard as the media makes it look. We do not have to be complicated, slam doors and hate our parents. I agree with him.

I mean some things you cannot stop, like developing a crush on a classmate, but you can control other things like arguing with your parents over the stupidest things because that's what is expected of every teenager.

Fund raisers

Coming to this school, I learned that there is always a way to help people. I remember my friends and I were looking at a Coach magazine, being the girls we are, so interested in fashion. We showed the magazine to our physics teacher, she looked at us and asked "How many died in the earthquake yesterday?"

We looked at her blankly trying to guess numbers.

She then told us to try and do something useful with our time and money to help those less fortunate rather than buying expensive things we will most likely get bored of soon.

So we planned for our senior year to have many fundraisers, hopefully successful organized ones.

Another person who plans to help us out is our Islamic Studies teacher.

We decided that with his help, we can organize a fundraiser in September or the beginning of October to help out the less fortunate. Being in this Islamic school has taught me to constantly think of people who are not as lucky as I am, to be able to buy what I want while they cannot buy what they need.

The June SAT scores come out in three days, and I am really scared. I am constantly thinking of my future, just like all my friends and students at school. I plan on applying for the dental program whether it is here or back in Egypt. The way I see it, I am never too far from my family. Here I have so many friends from school that have become part of my family.

I have been to their houses, spent hours at the mall with them, watched movies with them, and spent even more hours on the phone with them. In Egypt I have my family by blood, but I honestly do not know which relation is stronger; five years' worth of school, fun, sadness, failure and success, or blood relations?

I do know however that I plan on settling in Egypt after finishing college. I wish I had an inclination towards becoming a surgeon or a pediatrician or becoming some kind of scientist and curing diseases like cancer. But my dream has always been to become a dentist, and maybe I can help the less fortunate, poor people that need clean teeth too.

On Career Day, all the guests noticed that the middle school students and freshmen were concerned with the paycheck mostly. Growing in the Islamic system, the school has taught me something different. I have always wanted to become a dentist but why, I do not know.

Perhaps as a child it was for the title "Doctor." Then at one point, probably at the age of thirteen, it was for the money, but now I know it is about making a difference.

No, I do not like sounding too idealistic, but it is true. Imagine the happiness when you know you have made a difference in a person's life.

I have had the privilege of watching a less fortunate person's face light up when helped; or just watching them as they smile and wish you the best in life.

Money is important, but knowing you are a good person and loving yourself for it is priceless.

That is why I hope in ten years I will be working, helping people, perhaps attending social gatherings, researching and bringing back new medical discoveries to benefit my country.

I hope to become a Muslim Egyptian Dentist, not the other way around. I guess I am now convinced....as a friend once told me, constantly reminding me...everything happens for a reason.

#

Chapter Three: Senior Citizen 'Time' Capsule Traveler Searches for Core Identity in 1950 Coney Island

Senior Citizen # 1 speaks out in an essay of *therapeutic reminiscing* and *storytelling for closure*

Monologue for Performances:

Building a Dialogue Mirror to Speak to For Creating Terse Conversation

I still think of myself as a descendant of people who lived in ancient Greece and the old Greek islands and colonies. My paternal great grandmother born around 1834 in Bialystok, Poland, her daughter, A., *"The Cat"*--born around 1854, my dad, one of nine children born (last in birth order) in 1894, my mom, from another land, born in 1904, whom dad married in 1926, and I born before World War Two, all were and are tired of being beaten up for looking Jewish. We've had it.

We're not tailoring our noses or tinting our hair any more. We look Middle Eastern, and we are tired of Middle Eastern people, whatever their religion getting beaten up for looking like they just stepped out of Babylon or Beirut.

My mother looked like the actress, Joan Collins in the movie "The Egyptian." I look like the sultry Italian actress, Anna Magnani. We are all Mediterranean-type women descended from Neolithic farmers of the grain belt born from women who lived centuries in Bialystok, Poland, and we are tired of getting our ears boxed for not always looking like Swedish milk maids in spite of some of us born with red hair, light eyes, fair complexions, and freckles.

No matter how red our hair is or how green, blue, or hazel our eyes and light our skin, one look at our large, convex noses, and the shouts go up half in Yiddish, *"Favus, Favus, she gotta longa nuz."* (*Favus* sounds like *Vivus*, which in Latin means *alive* as in *"the baby lives" or life, a variation, perhaps of 'Lechaim,' which means "to life" as in a toast or a salutation.* Could the word have originated in early medieval Italy or France?)

So who enriched my tapestry? How many tribes are in my temporary container? At the cellular level I have a cultural and biological component. Why did those two components lead me to spend seven years in an Arab Jewish intermarriage to see how the other side lives? Why did I spend seven years disguised as an Arab housewife in a Brooklyn Jewish neighborhood and then in California? And why did I finally marry an Anglo-Saxon?

My journey was in search of a core identity, but it led to something transcending even that—a link with all peoples through universal archetypes. What made us what we are besides the changing climate?

The earliest tales my mother wove, starting about the age of three, was about when the German mothers boxed her ears. It wasn't in Europe, but in Albany, New York. My mother was born in an old house in Albany, New York in 1904 to a woman from Bessarabia, Romania, (Ashkenazic Jews and Germans migrated from Poland, Ukraine, Latvia, Belarus, Germany, and Lithuania to Bessarabia in the 18th century), and a blond, silver-eyed man who looked almost exactly like Clark Gable, from Lutsik, Ukraine.

Dad's parents came from Bialystok, Poland in the late 19th century. If I'm supposed to be so pink-and-white Polish, how come I look like I just stepped out of Beirut?

I'm probably mixed. How mixed, only my DNA says, and my maternal DNA says I'm Northern European, Southern European, and Middle Eastern or Iranic, yet closest to Armenian, old Anatolian, and Cypriot. So where's my core identity?

Do I look on the paternal side and try to guess how many genes I share with Arabs compared to Northern Europeans? Is it important? No, it is not as much as in finding my core identity. I'm looking instead for the cultural components of my DNA rather than solely the biological components. *I am what music heals me.*

When my mother was two years old, her parents divorced and her mother gave her away to her father. He took her to Philadelphia. There, she was raised by a redheaded stepmother from Vienna, Austria and Odessa, Russia. As I grew up, my mother would tell me story after story of how she was beaten by hate crimes in the U.S. as a child.

African-Americans beat her for having pink skin and silver eyes. Whites beat her for "looking Jewish" and having black and curly hair. And, gee, nobody beat her for looking like my mother. When she was ten in the fifth grade, she asked a fellow student, "Do I look Jewish?"

The student replied, "You got the map of Jerusalem printed on your face."

On and on, mom would talk to me, and each time, there was another tale of how she played with neighbor kids and their German mothers would box her ears and call her epithets with the word "Jew" in them.

The stereotype is of anyone from a Mediterranean country or the Caucasus Mountains who happens to have the profile of King Sargon of Babylon as his mask portrayed thousands of years ago, or a Sicilian profile with fair skin, light eyes, and dark hair. So why is it important? The Sicilian neighbors told her they thought she looked Sicilian. How does one look like a particular country? Is it an expression of the face? Clothing? Inclination of accent?

What's not symmetrical enough for you? Well neither was the profile of King Tut, or Pharaoh Ramses, (may his mummy rest in peace) and nobody puts his finger to his nose and curls it convexly, except in a 1971 "All in the Family" episode followed by familiar canned laughter.

My early childhood experienced World War II, in Brooklyn. We lived in a four-family house near Kings Highway. Between the ages of three and five, not only did mom tell me about the holocaust in Europe, because I was born in 1941, but she would rock me in her arms when I was three, sweating in anxiety, as she sang to me about the bombs that were coming to fall on New York pretty soon. There were lights out air raid drills, and always she told me the bombs were coming to fall, and they never did.

The sweating, the anxiety was there anyway, almost as if they had come. Then she'd tell me about how the Irish and German Americans used to beat her for looking Jewish in the neighborhoods. She grew up (aged 10 to 14) during World War One. The street we lived on had been mostly Jewish on one side and partly southern Italian on the other, and almost never the twain met or spoke to one another.

Mom was a battered wife. Not only did I experience the holocaust from her stories, but the battles inside my home. My father, age 47 when I was born, and my brother, 13 years older than I, beat mom. There were terrible fights. I hid in my room and drew cartoons of them fighting.

One day my father smashed my piano and violin and all my birthday toys because I kicked him out of the bed I slept in with my mother when he tried to enter the bed in the middle of the night to have sex with my mother.

I was nine, and I told him to get out. He slept in the room next door in twin beds with my older brother in the room. Men with men, women with women, throughout my parent's marriage. And he beat her. And she told me about how he beat her when she came home from the hospital with me a week old, and he punched her in the chest, and I fell from her arms into the snow. She had told him to hurry up and take the baby's picture because I was turning blue from the cold wind and snow.

My father always smashed things with hammers and axes. I was afraid someday he'd get me and kill me. Mom told me how much she worried, about everything, and most of all how awful it was to be Jewish and be beaten for looking Jewish. As I grew up, I began to look in the mirror and wonder whether I looked Jewish. I had a "Caspian Sea Nose."

My cousins told me "I looked very Semitic." So I began to make myself up to look like an ancient Egyptian, eye makeup, black wig or hair tint, and costume. As I grew into a teenager, I took up the Turkish Belly dance, the Egyptian cane dance, the Moroccan dance, and the *Zamba-Mora*, a mixture of Flamenco and Moorish. My ballet lessons started at the age of five. By the age of eleven I danced on point—(toe).

At nine I gave a performance in ballet, a solo on the stage at my elementary school. At seven I started violin lessons and at nine, piano lessons. Music became my life. At thirteen I added voice lessons. I went on to graduate from college as a creative writing major, fine art minor, with second minors in psychology and anthropology. I was into ethnomusicology and linguistics. My hobby was astronomy and illustration...writing poetry, novels.

Then, at 22, I took a train back from a vacation in Asbury Park, returning to New York. I was married at the time, to a non-Jew. It was 1964, and the movie, Cleopatra was all over town. I had tinted my hair black; made my eyes up to look Egyptian, and thought I looked like Liz Taylor when I gazed back at myself in the mirror. In August of 1964 I was married, two months pregnant, and then my self-image melted.

A man, who I call the neo-Nazi, told me not to cross between cars while the train was in motion until the train stopped in Elizabeth, New Jersey. He wasn't the conductor. He was a passenger with his wife. I couldn't understand why he would order me to "wait 'till the train stopped in Elizabeth." I told him I was pregnant and returning from the john, and needed to get back to my seat or my husband and mother riding in the next car would think I became ill in the bathroom. He ignored me.

So I passed in front of him to return to my seat. I didn't brush him or touch his luggage or anything. There was no conductor around, and normally the right procedure is when you walk from one train car to the next to use the bathroom, it's regular procedure to walk back to your seat in the next car by opening and closing the easily sliding doors.

There were no train rules broken, of course. Because I didn't defer and defied his command, by walking past him to reach the next car and return silently to my seat and husband, he grabbed my head in a vise-like grip with his hand and knee, squeezed, trying to crush my head between his knee and the wall of the train causing me great pain in the skull, and beat the hell out of me by squeezing my head. The pain of my head being squeezed first between his large hands and then between his knees was unbearable.

 Then he held me so I couldn't move and kicked me hard at the base of the spine while he yelled, "you dirty Jew." I went flying forward into the next car while his wife eyed my wedding ring as I faced her for a moment, and quietly smirked, "let her go, dear." She had the sweetest controlled voice as she looked up at me behind the fishnet veil of her pillbox hat.

The two reminded me of the painting, "Gothic American." He was bald, black hair around the rim of his ears, staring black eyes, pale skin. She looked the same with curled brown hair and wrinkles above her thin lips. The words, "dirty Jew," rang in my head. I walked back to my seat two cars down and never said a word to my husband or mother.

My husband would have returned and started a fight. My mother had just gotten out of the hospital and was recuperating. For the next twenty years I never said a word…to anyone. My fear of being Jewish went inward and increased. When I wrote about my experience, some women accused me of being "a man-hater."

The next day I stopped trying to look like Elizabeth Taylor in Cleopatra. I bleached the black tint out of my brown hair and made it bright red. With the freckles and hazel green eyes, I announced to the mirror that I now looked Welsh. Funny, how nobody noticed my convex nose, I surmised, when my hair was medium ash blonde or Killarney russet.

A few times during my teenage years in Brooklyn, some Puerto Ricans asked me whether I were Scottish or Irish. One black man tried to strangle me without asking what I was first. He only asked where my money was. A white man asked me once where the synagogue was, but I remember seeing him on TV as one of the skinheads taken into custody.

He was teasing me. First he asked me whether I needed help crossing the street and called me old lady. When I told him my age as if to say, I'm not that old, he brought up the Jewish lady part, emphatically with fury and frustration.

I was over age 60-something then and turned around and told him this face is what Mediterranean people look like. At that point in a public street in a Mexican area of San Diego, I was disgusted and just tired of people asking me where I'm from and what I am.

Every time I opened my mouth I was asked when I had come from New York. In one city, I walked into a seminar in Jewish history and heard that the professor had received death threats when he was appointed chairman of the Jewish Studies department that sponsored the free seminars at a university open to the public.

Most people who showed up were over age sixty and a few history students. So much for freedom of speech in a state university hall, it seems. The next lecture I went to was on quilting. The teacher never got any threats teaching crafts. All I went there for was to make a friend and find some place to belong. I still don't belong anywhere and have not yet made an attempt to make friends, although I want to. It became harder to find friends after age sixty-three, and I never learned to drive—too scared to take tests anymore.

It's more than forty years since I left Brooklyn. Why is it so important? I seldom speak in public, but talk to my video camera frequently. Then I let the videos become available to individuals seeking information.

 I've become a recluse to have some semblance of serenity. Better to be alone than to be 'pecked.' On the Internet people stop asking about my New York accent online. The silence of e-mail distracts them from even wanting to know. Interestingly enough, the man who beat me never bothered to ask first whether I was Jewish, Greek, or Armenian, or any other Eastern Mediterranean national or descended from, thereof, because we all look alike to him, but he singled out "Jew" and beat me for looking Jewish. I am an American with parents born in New York State.

What is Jewish supposed to look like, an Assyrian king of 3,500 years ago? Why do most Assyrian Christians look so much like me? With whom does my DNA cluster? Why can't we all accept one another's diversity without asking, without making it so important to know what someone's core identity is in privacy. I'm not your egg donor, so why ask? Nearly each time I open my mouth someone asks me when I left New York. I've been out of New York since 1965.

The man on the train who beat me didn't ask my name or look to see whether I wore a cross or a star or anything else. For a moment I wanted to say, "I'm Maltese. This is the face of Malta, or Naples, or Istanbul, or Crete." Perhaps my 38 college units in anthropology would have come in handy at that moment. But I said nothing for decades after that event.

So scared was my mother of being Jewish that she first joined the Dutch reformed Protestant church in Brooklyn and took me there when I was nine. We landed in the Unitarian church for decades. I also went to many other churches in the neighborhood. At the Catholic Church, the nun once said to me, "I don't think you're Catholic. You look Jewish. What's your name?" I replied, "Angelica," because we lived near an Italian/Sicilian neighborhood, and I used to ask my Christian friends to donate their old rosaries to me because I collected them for those who needed them.

I learned my "hail Mary's" and pinned up all the rosaries in our basement where I lit a candle on Shabbat and prayed in Hebrew and in English, both the Catholic "hail Mary's" and the Jewish

Sabbath blessing prayer every Friday night. I spoke to Jesus and anyone else listening and asked a lot of philosophical questions, and wrote a book of prayers when I was nearly twelve.

Then I started reading Tibetan Buddhism and all about reincarnation from other religions, including the Eastern religions. I saw religion as links on a chain knowing we all come from and go to the same place. A loving God would not have created people in the first place unless he, she, or it, the Creator or designer sent us to the same place equally and took us from that place to be born again and again.

I wondered who wrote the Bible with all those inconsistencies and contradictions, but thought it was great to have all that control over people who really would do you wrong, and freedom to choose for all the people seeking for the highest right for the good of all.

I ended up at age 21 marrying a 26-year old man who called himself an Arab Sheik. He worked as a machinist before he opened his business, a restaurant which soon closed. When I was pregnant, he beat the hell out of me. The marriage ended after six and a half years, when I became a battered wife, and he took my two children to Syria where his mother and six brothers reared them after he divorced me and took away all the money in the bank, my furniture, and threw me out into the street after more than 6 years of marriage. At 33 I married a Protestant man, American, half German, and half English. We are now married more than 30 years. I can't think of anyone who loves me, except my cat.

He used to beat me too, but far less than the Sheik, mostly more verbally, but twice a year physically, but now he's only verbally abusive and beats me only once a year if he can catch me when I run from him. He beats me only when we are moving from one house to another, and he's stressed. He has intermittent explosive disorder to some degree, low serotonin levels, and explodes when he doesn't get his way, like when he wanted some old bookcases for fifty dollars, and I wanted something new.

I'm still married to him. He never reads what I write, and I write under different names. When he quiets down, he's back to his old withdrawn cold fish self just like daddy. We have not shared the same room for almost 30 years, his choice first, not mine, but now his snoring is loud enough to cause me insomnia. I've been celibate since 1976. He has no affection for me, but I don't have to pay rent. That's great as I don't have an income although I'd love an income. He says give me a break. I say give me a connection.

A wife isn't supposed to complain about her cold-fish husband according to etiquette, but I'm a woman who can't take care of herself married to a man who can't take care of a wife. He's a commanding, bullying, whining and volcanic explosive with low serotonin levels, high narcissism and worry about self-image. I'm shy, frightened, old, and spent, but I like the free rent, the backyard, and my doggies who do show me affection by wagging their tails when I give them their food and a hug.

My both husbands became emotionally abusive dads to me, just like my own dad, but since my present husband abuses me far less than the first husband did, I'll stay as long as there's money to pay the taxes on the house and keep food in the fridge.

 I married my first husband at 21, the Sheik because I thought in a previous life, I had come from Egypt or Syria, but digging deeper, I found at that at 13 I was secretly in love with a Syrian Jewish boy in my class because he was rich, lived in a private house on Ocean Parkway, and was handsome.

A clique of Syrian Jewish girls said I could join
their 8th grade sorority if I took all my clothes
off in front of them and let their 6-year old
brother feel me up. Wanting so bad to join their
clique, I went into the closet and took off all my
clothes. The girls grabbed my clothes, tossed
them over my head, playing monkey in the
middle, and humiliated me.

Then they pushed me out of their house and
into the gutter with me barely missing the path
of an oncoming car by inches. I was totally
intimidated and humiliated. Thereafter, I never
had a friend for years.

Later, I tried making friends with a Jewish girl.
She was rich, an Ashkenazi, and became my
best friend. But she betrayed me like the
others. When I confided in her, making her like
a sister, that my mom was arrested for
shoplifting and I was so shocked, she turned
around and made up a lie that I had stolen her
empty purse. Her mother called my brother and
screamed about my mother being a shoplifter.
She never knew my mother. I didn't take her
purse and never would have thought such
thoughts.

All I wanted to be is accepted by the rich, or
those richer than I was. Her father practiced
law. Mine was a janitor and 8th-grade dropout,

born in 1894 in New York. She kept asking me to return the purse. I kept asking why she'd make up such as story and then tell her mother about my mother, or why her mother would call my older brother and rub his nose in the dirt that my mother was arrested for shoplifting, when I had told her daughter this in confidence as my best friend.

Needless to say, I have no friends today, no living relatives beyond my distant children that I know of, and a husband who puts me down verbally, teases me, and sometimes batters me. People seem to have betrayed me a lot. And yet, I still hope someday I'll find a friend. I'm no longer *sociophobic*. Nor do I walk through life totally alone any more. I can choose joining associations or meditating in isolation, usually home-based. I spend many days reading and writing or walking through the zoo.

One freedom I cherish. It's to belong to several religions at one time and to attend all the churches, synagogues, or other houses of worship that I want—usually the Unitarian. I go to Christian churches on Christian holidays and to Jewish synagogues on Jewish holidays.

I want my freedom to choose any religion anytime and to attend any celebration of life. I cherish this freedom because I believe God is love and that we all come from and go to the same place. No creator creates any intelligent being unequal to any other intelligent being on any universe. And our companion pets come with us into eternity and give us comfort.

For a decade I was housebound with agoraphobia and panic between age 23 and 33. It burned itself out without any treatment, as I was penniless. Today, I have two computers, a paid-off home, and it's all his. I'm still too scared to tell anyone I'm Jewish, except other Jews. I belong to the Unitarian church, and I still celebrate, alone, the Jewish holidays.

My two children are devout Muslims, still trying to convert me to Islam and talking about Jews at the same time, warning me not to tell their friends that I'm Jewish. I smile to their face. I'm forbidden to tell my grandchildren my religion. What religion? I'm one with the universe because we all come from and go back to the exact same place. I'll read the book or Bible of any religion and contemplate all the good points.

Why am I scared to be Jewish? The Skinheads and Neo Nazis are all over this town. I am respected in the Unitarian church. I give donations to the Jewish organizations. Secretly, I sneak off to "Chabad" and dance with the

"Hassid," clapping my hands in joy. On Christmas I'm in the Unitarian church listening to the fine carols and playing them on my organ in a celebration of life.

And I still belly dance to Middle Eastern music when I'm alone at home. I love all peoples and cherish their music as a divine gift to humankind. In soothing music from all cultures I find the harmony and serenity of healing.

My mother always said that someday there's going to be another holocaust right here in America and they'll get me if I tell anyone I'm Jewish. I really don't know when or if that might happen. I pray not. I cherish the freedom of religion and the separation of church and state.

Taking away one's freedom of worship is akin to being told you have the wrong country's nose and that a surgeon must take off what identifies you. It's like being told that thousands of years ago an ancestor came from a certain place and that has to be corrected.

A plastic surgeon once said he'd take the hump off my nose, but what's the point? I don't need symmetry to feel beautiful on the outside or inside. I need the experience of joyful song. I hope no more mayhem will happen, hope so much that I pray tensely with my eyelids squeezed shut.

The only thing I can do about it is to try to make the world a kinder and gentler place, being the idealist that I am as I do my housewifely crafts and write a novel a year to keep active.

I go to the Unitarian church and hold my head up high, and I go to the synagogue and hold my head up high, and I don't want anybody calling me ethnic names or hating me because my great-great grandparents practiced a particular religion in a country I've never seen.

My favorite author is Ray Bradbury. We all see things, not the way they are, but the way we are. A hate crime doesn't have to play on stage where observers can distance themselves. Fear doesn't have to take top billing publicly; it can be internal.

When will it be okay anywhere in the world to follow your spiritual meditations privately and not be chastised publicly for your symmetry or hue?

How are we all doing with visual shorthand? I have not "gotten a life." Instead, I've learned to forgive others and myself.

Why would a nice, Jewish girl from near Coney Island marry an Arab Sheik and live disguised as an Arab housewife first in a Jewish section of Brooklyn and then in a multi-ethnic section of Brooklyn, for nearly seven years?

Maybe because we all come from and go to the same place or maybe because in a former life I was both, maybe I'm looking for something beyond a core identity, or maybe I just want a connection to everyone else in the world, but on a higher plane that reaches beyond territory and tribe to universal archetypes.

Everything ever written available today is humankind-made. I get the feeling that everything ever written or designed reflects only human recombination of mind, body, and achievement.

After all, you get to the universal only through the concrete details with which we all identify across cultures. Everyone on the planet is connected by a common ancestor.

I'm connected to the three fellows who lived somewhere in the Middle East 7,800 years ago, the woman who lived in Europe 20,000 years ago, and the rest who left the Fertile Crescent, Central Asia, Africa, or India between 60,000 and 30,000 years ago for better campgrounds.

They are all connected to me by my DNA and love of art, music, and writing. And the most profound connection there can be outside of family and friends is the unconditional love and loyalty of one's dog to the human pack—at least for the next million years.

We are too close to the cave and a billion years in evolution too far from controlling nature's response to us and our response to what's out there waiting.

After all, we move from energy to matter and back to energy and then to matter again and again forever.

So we might as well laugh and enjoy it until we evolve far enough to harness it. It always has been part of a very special Internet connection called communication for sharing meaning. We are all about connections.

#

Chapter Four:

Evidence

Writing Plays for High-School Students, Families, and Mature Adults from Life Stories and Personal Histories: Working with the Evidence

Family stories are evidence of who we are. 'Salable' life stories usually are launched in the media—the major national press of credible repute—before they are produced as a video or movie and published as a book. Personal histories, like corporate histories may end up as time capsules on disk and on Web sites as video and audio documentaries or in books.

Time capsules may contain personal histories, corporate histories, and even DNA-driven genealogy reports along with keepsake memorabilia. Material is documented on video, audio, and in text format. It's truly a multimedia production. Oral history tapes are transcribed and archived in libraries and museums. Here's how to document your personal history and launch a salable life story.

Write and produce as a video or audio your personal or oral history. Or present a folkloric tradition. Your salable life story can be presented as a time capsule, disk, Web site and keepsake album. The format may be a dramatic script, book, article, story, skit, radio broadcast, diary, novel, letter, article, monologue, or poem.

Or cut and paste the text file into synthetic voice software and have it read and saved in your computer in most languages or with selected male or female voices or regional accents. Then 'burn' it to a DVD, flash drive, or any other format. Or stream it as a video and audio file. Your life story is now saved in multimedia as a time capsule.

Before you think about publishing your life story or anyone else's, launch the personal history in the media. If you are working with someone else's life story, you'll need a signed release form allowing you to put the story on your Web site and/or on disk.

Be sure your form releases you from liability resulting from someone else's name going public for educational and scholarly research. Start with your own personal history and learn what pitfalls to avoid. Gain insight, foresight, and hindsight.

Personal and oral history taping and archiving also branches into fields such as folklore and oral tradition, anthropology and ethnology. A personal historian can be an employee or an independent contractor. You can transcribe oral history tapes or work with creating audio and video files from your already written book or story.

Write Plays for Junior and Senior High-School Students or Senior Citizens

So you want to write a life story as a play or monologue? You are worth the storage. Launch your own personal history business by first doing a personal history on yourself and members of your family. You can include corporate histories, success story case histories, and life story writing circles for individuals. When somebody asks you for the facts, the primary source for research on your life story, only you can supply the evidence. This evidence is valuable. It's all about who you are, what you stand for, and how you reached out to others.

Showcase your own life history for your family, friends, or historians. Your life story is valuable now and in the distant future. You are part of history. Make sure a release form goes into your time capsule with your multimedia wishes concerning your life story in any format.

Maybe you'd also like to make time capsules? What about including DNA-driven genealogy reports as keepsake memorabilia? Include life stories, genealogy records, oral traditions, and folkloric customs. What's more valuable than a life story?

You can focus on intergenerational writing, autobiographies, diaries, journals, video biographies, oral histories, corporate histories, tales, oral history tape transcribing. Or concentrate on life story writing in the form of books, video, audio, Web sites, skits, poems, memoirs, creative writing, greeting card discs, DVDs, streaming, drives, and various formats of video productions. Transfer your older tapes from twenty years ago to discs or drives. Design Web video broadcasting or make time capsules.

Write your own personal history. How do you write and launch salable life stories in the media, in the publishing world, and in the world of video, multimedia, Internet multicasting, Web-based historical documentaries, life-story-based novels, and film?

Every life story has four seasons and twelve stages like the months in a year. The four seasons are infancy, childhood, adulthood, and grace-age. Or you want to be an oral traditionalist, folklorist, or oral historian, folklore librarian, or archivist and conservator of old videos, photos, letters, articles, disks, and books. What makes your personal history salable?

Marketability is born in the national media. Credible journalism launches your story to agents, entertainment attorneys, publishers and producers long before your book is published or your video is made available to the public through your Web site, DVD, CD greeting card, or other time capsule.

Maybe you want to know how to promote and publicize life stories in the media before they are published as books or produced cinematically. Or you want to write, promote, and sell your autobiography—commercially—to a selected niche market audience.

Personal histories are found in books, video, film, audio, and games. Depending upon your field of focus, your autobiography or anyone else's life story can become a salable personal history. A life story becomes 'commercial' or salable when it is launched in the national press before it is published as a book or produced as a movie or video.

It also can become a time capsule on disk and/or on an Internet Web site. An audio or video tape on the Web is part of a personal broadcasting network. Personal and corporate histories are time capsules. Oral histories may be transcribed into text.

Text writings may be imported or cut and pasted into synthetic voice software and quickly turned into audio files, DVDs, CDs, drives, or other formats as technology changes, and uploaded to a Web site to be broadcast much like a personal radio station or broadcasting network.

Audio or video files can be uploaded to Web sites and download to personal computers anywhere in the world with Internet access. The files can be saved by right-clicking a computer mouse and "saved as a target" in anyone's computer and then played on a computer hard disk drive or saved to other disks or transferred to most any media formats.

Live voices or synthetic software voices can read text and be saved as a computer file much the same as any audio or video file. And to make sure text stays as readable text, books of all sizes or skits and plays or scripts can be written or transcribed from oral interviews of anyone's life story.

The same may be done for the oral history of a corporation, or for folklore tradition. It's all part of a career as a personal and/or oral historian. Here, anthropology, history, ethnology, creative writing, genealogy, and public speaking combine. You can even put printouts and reports of DNA-driven genealogy research on a person or family in a genealogy-related time capsule to be opened by future generations.

In the time capsule could be video and audio material, text writings, diaries, oral traditions, and anything related to life story writing. Keepsakes and poetry, dramatizations, skits, plays, and the reminiscing of individuals, groups, or corporations may go into a time capsule. What used to be keepsake albums (scrapbooks) can now become time capsules.

If you want to be a personal historian, you can open an independent business where you travel in an area in order to 'videotape' people with your camcorder, usually in digital high 8 format, and transcribe the tapes to appear as text transcripts of what they said orally on the video or audio tape, CD, or DVD.

You can spend up to six hours transcribing a one-hour video or audio tape. Often there are two voices, the interviewer and the interviewee on the tape. Some people may want to speak into a tape recorder or camcorder and tape themselves when they are alone in a room without an interviewer. These people would receive a list of questions to look at so they can answer focusing on turning points or highlight the significant events in their lives.

You may want to tape a group of people speaking for five to seven minutes each on a special topic such as what did you do during

World War II? Maybe the people in the group would describe what it was like living in a certain place during a certain decade or working in a certain environment or occupation.

Life story tapes usually run about an hour for individuals to talk about their entire life history in five minute segments. Fifteen five-minute segments can bring them up to age seventy-five. These can be taped weekly or daily during a fifteen-week 'semester' or fifteen days of daily taping where they speak in five-minute 'chunks' on one videotape.

 The five minute segments allows art work, photos, slides, or video clips of other scenes, such as the house they live in or anything pertinent to be taped or photographed and edited in between segments. A personal history taping can run as a 15-week class in life story writing. For those who don't want to appear on camera, audio tape can be used in a tape recorder.

Most people find it difficult to sit in front of a camcorder for one hour and continuously speak or answer questions. Some enjoy an interview that does last an hour. Others would rather use the five-minute segments and have you tape them in a classroom setting or their home another day, perhaps each day at the same time during a 15-week 'semester.'

Personal history may be done as an adult education course in any type of setting from recreation room of an assisted living facility or senior community center to a private home or public classroom in an adult education class in life story writing. If you're running a class, you might have the people meet from 11 am to noon each Sunday, perhaps right after their 10 am church service for a recording.

Each person can spend as much time as he or she wants—either one five-minute segment or perhaps three segments totaling fifteen minutes each week until the one-hour tape is completed. You can include, if desired, a DNA-driven genealogy report in case the person wants a DNA test for ancestry to put into a time capsule for family members and future generations.

The time capsule would contain a text version of the life story of each member of the family or of one individual. It would also have a video tape, an audio tape, any keepsakes, and the creative work such as poetry or skits and writings or art work, photos, and other memorabilia that can fit into the time capsule.

A video or audio tape would also be preserved on a DVD and a CD, and if possible, uploaded to a Web site as a video and/or audio file of the individual or one of the family members who has access to the Internet and can purchase Web site space allowing a video and audio file to be uploaded along with the text transcription or life story writing of the individual. This makes a wonderful time capsule gift in personal history.

 You'll want to know how to write it so that it can be marketed to your niche customers or audience. Maybe you'll combine your personal history with a practical invention of some type, such as an inexpensive device everyone can use or a special cooking utensil. This book is about becoming a personal historian. From there, your works can diverge into many roads or branches that link back to personal history.

Why do you want to write a personal history of someone or an autobiography of yourself and make it commercial to sell to a niche or wide audience? You may want to flummox the readers and enhance their public or private lives.

You may want to protect an institution from mockery. Or you want to take a stand and speak in codes that are the shorthand of living. To be concrete, writing and/or producing or transcribing personal history, oral history, folklore and oral tradition may focus on taking a stand on specific areas of life such as recording your experience being bullied in elementary school and focusing on taking a stand by writing a series of teaching guides with a training videotape or disk featuring your personal history and the personal histories of others with similar past experiences.

Maybe you want to join your personal history with others' personal histories in a documentary disk or tape defending a symbol of religious or ethnic identity. Should you wear that symbol in public, for example, in school or at work or during travel?

Should you defend that symbol with a time capsule, an oral history, or personal history videotape, DVD, and text material? On your Web site in multimedia? In a keepsake album?

 In what do you seek comfort? Your personal history can be about seeking comfort in food, work, play, care giving, leisure, travel, research, art, writing, or whatever you choose. What's your crusade about and how would you describe or show your slogan?

If you write a commercial autobiography, you'll want to know how to market your work. You might wish to make time capsules to preserve the highlights of life stories of older adults or corporations. You can carve out a career as a personal historian and interview people, record what they say on a variety of media, and have the tapes transcribed to text or transcribe them yourself.

You can conserve paper or videos, transfer the medium to newer technology formats, or make keepsake albums and multimedia time capsules. 'Scrap booking' is about making **Keepsake Albums,** and can become oral tradition or personal history as a play or skit.

What you're creating are keepsakes or time capsules. And what is a keepsake to the average person becomes a time capsule to an oral historian and archaeologist. You can even include DNA-driven genealogy reports in a keepsake or time capsule.

 Maybe you want to write commercial biographies or your autobiography. Perhaps you'll ghostwrite other people's autobiographies. Or you'll perhaps choose to write corporate biographies and success stories and be a case history manager or consultant for new companies. You can transcribe oral histories. Another route is to produce or tape video biographies and archive them in oral history libraries, usually at universities, museums, or other foundation.

\#

Chapter Five:

What Makes a Personal History or Life Story Highlight Salable as a Play or Skit?

Q. What makes a life story saleable?

A. Buzz appeal. High velocity personal memoir. A life story is salable when it has universal appeal and identity. An example is a single parent making great sacrifices to put bread on the table and raise a decent family in hard times. Many people identify with the universal theme of a life story. Buzz appeal draws in the deep interest of the press to publicize and lend credibility to a life story, to put a spin on it in the media, and to sell it to the public because all readers may be able to see themselves in your life story.

Q. To whom do you sell your life story?

A. You sell your life story to publishers specializing in life stories. If you look under biographies in a book such as Writer's Guide to Book Editors, Publishers, and Literary Agents,

1999-2000, by Jeff Herman, Prima Publishing, you'll see several pages of publishers of life story, biography, and memoirs or autobiography.

A few include The Anonymous Press, Andrews McMeel Publishing, Applause Theatre Book Publishers, Barricade Books, Inc., Baskerville Publishers, and many more listed in that directory. Also take a look at Writers Market, Writers Digest Books, checkout Memoirs in the index. Publishers include Feminist Press, Hachai, Hollis, Narwhal, Northeastern University Press, Puppy House, Westminster, John Knox, and others. Check categories such as creative nonfiction, biography, ethnic, historical, multicultural and other categories for lists of publishers in your genre. Don't overlook writing your life story as a play, monologue, or script or for the audio book market.

Q. How do you present your life story in order to turn it into a saleable book, article, play, or other type of literature so that other people will want to read it?

A. You write a high-velocity powerful personal memoir that *emphasizes cultural criticism and theory*. Or you write a factual expose, keep a journal on the current cultural pulse, or write a diary about what it feels like to be single and dating in your age group--thirty something, sixty-something, or whatever you choose. You become an investigative biographer. You write a riveting love story. Or how to use love to heal. Or you write about breaking through old barriers to create new publishing frontiers.

Q. How do you write a commercial biography?

A. Make sure someone wants to buy it before you write the whole thing. The details will be forthcoming in the course as it begins. Then contact the press, reporters in the media with credibility who write for a national daily newspaper or reputable magazine. Also contact radio and cable TV stations to do interviews on a selected event in your life story or biography. Pick a niche market where the particular audience has a special interest in that experience.

Q. What's the difference between authorized and unauthorized?

A. Authorized means you have permission and approval from the person about whom you're writing.

Q. Who gets assigned to write biographies of celebrities or other famous people?

A. Usually newspaper columnists who cover the beat or subject area, or you're a known writer who contacts an agent specializing in writing or ghostwriting celebrity biographies. You can enter this profession from many doors. I'll explain in the course.

#

Writing Your Ending First Gives You Closure And Clues How To Solve The Problems In Your Life Story. Teaching Life Story Writing Online

When you write a salable life story, it's easier to write your ending first. Eventually, with experience working with a variety of life stories, you can start quality circles or classes in life story writing (writing your salable memoirs, autobiography, biography, corporate history, family history, your diary as a commercial novel or play or true confession, true story, or true crime book or story or script).

Also, you can teach life story writing, interviewing, or videobiography on the Internet for yourself or for an existing school or program. It's relaxing and comforting to sit at home in perfect quiet and type a lecture into a screen browser such as the courses that can be offered through www.blackboard.com and other programs.

Or teach online using a live chat screen. Customize your course to the needs of your students. You may need certification or a graduate degree to teach for a university online, but there's also adult education classes given in nontraditional settings such as churches, libraries, and museums.

Online, you can offer independent classes and go into business for yourself as a personal historian. Another way is to offer time capsules, keepsake albums, gift baskets, greeting cards, life stories on video, DVD, or transcribed from oral history. Work with libraries, museums, or your own independent classes.

You can work at home or be mobile and travel to other people's homes or senior centers and assisted living recreation rooms, community centers, or schools and theaters to work with life stories. Some companies have put life-story recording kiosks in public places such as train stations or airports.

You may wish to view the *StoryCorps* site online at http://www.storycorps.net/. I highly recommend these websites. Or you may wish to find your own mission or purpose and create your own business recording the life stories of a variety of people in video, sound, text, or multimedia formats. You also may wish to check

out the Story Corps Facebook page at:
https://www.facebook.com/StoryCorps/.

One revelation you may have is that your life story isn't only for your family and friends anymore. As part of history, the world can now experience the one universal that connects us--life, and within a life story--insight, foresight, and hindsight.

Maybe writing for reminiscence is part of the time-capsule generation that emphasizes the how, where, why, and what of your life story because every life has value, is worth a book, video, or play, and needs to be preserved as part of history for future generations to see.

Diaries of senior citizens are in demand. To sell them, you need buzz appeal, visibility in the press for writing simple stories of how you struggled to put bread on the table and raised a family alone, or what you've learned from your mistakes or experiences, how you solved problems, gave yourself more choices, grew, and came to understand why you were transformed. People are looking for universal experiences to help them make decisions.

Start by finding a newspaper reporter from a publication that is well-respected by the public, and have that person write about your life story experience or what you do with other peoples' life stories as a personal historian. That's the first step to introducing a 'salable' life story.

The technique differs from writing a life story like a first-person diary novel for only your family and/or friends. With a 'salable' life story, you write about the universal experiences that connect all of us. If readers or viewers can identify with what you have to say, your words open doors for them to make decisions and choices by digesting your information.

The Proliferation of Playwriting Courses Online Targets Writing Your Life Story

The sheer number of classes on the Internet is like an explosion of education. You can now earn a master's degree in the techniques of teaching online from some universities that offer these courses through their continuing education department. Check out some of the display ads in a variety of magazines of interest to writers. How many writing courses online are offered?

How do you develop *buzz appeal*, pre-sell your book, and encourage press coverage of reminiscence writing, before you send your work to a publisher or agent or self-publish your memoirs, life story highlights, or reminiscence writing and/or storytelling? A few years ago diaries as books were "in" just like several years before that the books about angels were "in style." What will be next?

Back in the year 2000, what enthralled readers included simple stories on how single parents put bread on the table, reared a family, and learned from their mistakes. What will be big in the future in publishing will be simple tales of what you learned, how you came to understand, and what you'll share with readers because what you learned from my mistakes helped you to grow and become a better person making the world a gentler place. Those books will be about values, virtues, and ethics in simple stories that help people heal. It will be universal stories with which we all can identify and use to solve problems and make decisions.

 By the following year books showed readers how to have more choices and find more alternative solutions, more possibilities, and to find more information with which to solve problems and make decisions. A lot of those books will come from salable diaries and life stories as well as corporate histories and executive histories.

What was hot by 2002 was how people escaped domestic violence and made better choices through education and creativity enhancement. By 2003-2004 books focused on creativity enhancement and self-expression. The year 2003 became a utopia for books on creativity enhancement through personal experience and life story. You only have to look at the book lists in the publisher's magazines to see what the fad is for any one year and interview publishing professionals for the trends and directions for the following year.

Write about the human side of careers worked at for years. What did you retire to? How did you survive historic events, rear your family, or solve problems?

The purpose *of personal history writing* can be, among other goals, **to find closure**. Those who can't use a hand-operated mouse and need to use a foot pedal mouse, breath straw, or other devices can still operate computers. Others need assistance software to magnify the screen or audio software such as "Jaws," to hear as they type on keyboards for writers who are visually impaired.

The idea is to use personal history and life story writing as a healing instrument to make contact with others, find this closure, relieve stress, to talk to parents long gone, to make decisions on how to grow, find understanding, learn from past mistakes, grow, and become a better person in one's own eyes.

Other students take a personal history, oral history, or life story writing classes to pass on to their grandchildren a script, a novel, a story, or a collage of their life experiences, and still others want corporate histories of how they founded their companies and became role models of success for business students to simulate, how they became successful giants for others to follow and benchmark.

Still other students are visionaries who want their life stories to be used to enhance the creativity of readers. Some of my students want to write their life story as a computer or board game on how they solved their own problems that are universal to all of us. And you have students who want careers as personal historians recording, transcribing, and preserving in a variety of formats the personal histories of individuals, families, corporations, art forms, and institutions.

Some are into conservation of videos, photographs, text material, tape recordings, CDs, DVDs, and other multimedia formats. All are involved in making time capsules for future researchers, historians, scholars, librarians, genealogists, and specialists who research personal and oral history or specialized history, such as music and art or rare books and manuscripts. Others are collectors. Most want a time capsule of a relative, complete with not only a relative's keepsake albums or video diary, but sometimes even a DNA printout for ancestry.

If you look in many publications of interest to writers, you might see online or correspondence courses offered to writers at American College of Journalism, Burlington College, Columbus University, specialists in distance education, or at Gotham Writers' Workshops at www.WritingClasses.com. There's also Writers Digest University at the website: https://www.writersonlineworkshops.com/. And there are data bases where you can learn about agents. These are some of the online classes in writing that are advertised.

Check out the program that meets your individual writing and/or speaking needs. You'll also see ads for classes in personal story writing in publications for writers and storytellers.

 You can get paid to teach what you love to do so much--share your writing techniques and write. Some writing schools online may put articles up on their trade journal online. And you can always sell articles to paying markets and use the clips with resumes. Thanks to the Internet--even a disabled teacher who isn't able to speak before a class for health reasons or drive to class, can teach and write online.

Personal history writing courses could also aim to show research on how creative writing can heal or have therapeutic qualities in gentle self-expression and quality circles online, and now I've found students who learn how to write a life story as therapy to heal and to find closure, solve problems, and to explore more choices, alternatives, and growth towards a kinder and gentler world.

You can focus strictly on recording, transcribing, and archiving people's or corporation's personal or oral histories and preserving them in a variety of formats as time capsules or target the more creative end of teaching writing personal histories as books, plays, or skits. In other words, you can be both a personal historian and a writing coach or focus on either career or business—oral and personal historian, or teacher of courses or "quality circles" in writing autobiographies and biographies for commercial markets.

You can start private classes on a mailing list and chat board. A fair price to charge could be about $80 per student for advanced workshops in writing salable material for 4-week courses with a 10-page critique per student. Your aim would be to be an online job coach in a writing or personal history career. Help students find ways to get into print by referring you them to resources. Show how to make writing more commercial. Reveal the techniques of effective story writing in your true story, biography, memoirs, autobiography, diary, journal, novel, story, play, or article.

A lot of biography writing is focused on interviews, whereas writing a diary or monologue focuses on inner reflections and expressions in explaining how you came to understand, learn from your past mistakes or experiences and good choices, and share how you solved problems, grew, and changed or were transformed.

Personal diaries start out with poetic-like descriptions of the senses, with lines that are detailed and factual, terse and to the fact or writing that's poetically-chiseled writing such as the following:

Writing creative nonfiction poetically as reminiscence therapy

"Cat shadow plump I arrive, carrying my Siamese kitten like a rifle through a forested

landscape, while the only sensation I feel is fur stretched like flaxen wires and the tote bag where my new kitten, Patches, hangs on. A gentle clock, the red beams of light reflected in the feline's blue eyes remind me that it's time for both of us to eat. His claws dig into my purse strap like golden flowers curling in redwood trees. I inhale his purrs near lemon blossoms, warm as the cat's high-pitched meow that flowed between the mist-soaked branches."

Have an enriching writing experience. I truly believe writing heals in some ways. It's a transformative experience like meditation or having the comforting feeling of watching a waterfall in natural settings or sitting in a garden of hanging green plants.

Writing recharges my energy must like petting my kitten, Kokowellen, a Siamese while sitting in an orchid garden listening to soothing melodies.

You might want to critique for pay, the pages of other people's writing of personal histories if they want to write for the commercial markets.

In that case, critiquing may be done by email and online. That way they don't send any hard copy to mail back or get lost. Keep a copy.

You may wish to teach online a course with the critique, as you'll get far more for your $80 for each ten pages of critiquing as a fair price, plus the tuition of the course as perhaps another $80. Or charge what market rate is in your area.

A course may provide resources, techniques, and ways to revise your material that helps you gain visibility. It's important to pre-sell your book and gain publicity for your writing before you send it off to a publisher or agent. You'll want to know how not to give too much away, but how to attract positive attention so people will eagerly look forward to hearing more from you.

Keep a separate mailing list for your online students. Make a mailing list. Plays or monologues written from memoirs and diaries or excerpts and highlights of life stories are in right now in the publishing world. It's not a passed fad, yet, like the angel books were a decade ago. If you're writing a diary, you want to write something in your first or second page after the opening that may read like this to be more commercial:

"Eagerness to learn grows on me. I see it reflected in the interviewers who stare at me, their enthusiasm is an approval of my expansive mind. I read so much now, just to look at the

pages is to feel nourished. A kind of poetry turns into children's books on DVDs like a stalk that grows nowhere else is in season.

Creativity, like color, runs off my keyboard into the cooking water of my screen, drenched in pungent brainstorming. Writing online puts me in every farmer's kitchen. My computer has a good scent, and the stories written on its screen are apples bursting on the trees of my fingers. On my Web site, photos hang like lanterns. Teaching online ripens my stories. I analyze what effective storytelling means. Picture in three dimensions, pagodas of the mind."

If you come across writers block, try writing the lyrics to a song as a way to start writing your life story

You don't need to read notes, just fiddle with the words based upon an experience in time. Start by writing the ending first. Perhaps your title on salable diaries could be, "Pretty Little Secret," or "Ending the Silence," or "Results of Promises," or "Guided by a Child's Silence," or "Unraveling a Tale," or "Bravery and Unspeakable Links," or "Unveiled, Unbridled, Unbound." My title was "Insight, Hindsight, and Foresight."

#

Chapter Six:

"Celebration of Life" Plays and Skits Based on Interviewing and Recording Personal History

People are "less camera shy" when two from the same peer group or class pair up and interview each other on video camcorder or on audio tape from a list of questions rehearsed. People also can write the questions they want to be asked and also write out and familiarize themselves with the answers alone and/or with their interviewers from their own peer group.

Some people have their favorite proverbs, or a logo that represents their outlook on life. Others have their own 'crusade' or mission. And some have a slogan that says what they are about in a few words...example, "seeking the joy of life," or "service with a smile."

A play can come from someone's slogan, proverb, or motto for example. A slogan, logo, proverb, or motto (or even a logo) can form the foundation for a questionnaire on what they want to say in an oral history or personal history video or audio tape on in a multimedia presentation of their life story highlights. Here are some ways to interview people for personal history time capsules or how to inspire them to interview one another in a group setting or in front of a video camcorder in private with only interviewer and interviewee present.

And then there are those who want to tape themselves alone in their room or office with a camcorder on a tripod and a remote control device or a tape recorder and photographs. When records stop, there are always the DNA-driven genealogy and ancestry printouts.

Some people enjoy writing their life stories more than they like to speak about it. Or they prefer to read from a script as an audio tape. For those whose voices are impaired or for those who prefer to let a synthetic software voice tell their story, I recommend software such as TextAloud. This software allows anyone to cut and paste their writing from a disk such as a floppy disk, CD, DVD, or hard drive disk to the TextAloud software and select the type of voice to read their writing. With AT&T Natural Voices, you can select a male or female voice.

There are also voices with accents, such as a British accent male voice, and voice software available in a variety of languages to read writing in other languages. TextAloud is made by Nextup.com at the Web site: http://www.nextup.com/. According to their Web site, "TextAloud MP3 is Text-to-Speech software that uses voice synthesis to create spoken audio from text. You can listen on your PC or save text to MP3 or wave files for listening later." I play the MP3 files on my MP3 player.

I save the audio files to an external drive as MP3 files. In this way I can turn my writing into audio books, pamphlets, or articles, poetry, plays, monologues, skits, or any form of writing read aloud by the synthetic software voice software. I save my audio files as MP3 files so I can play my personal history audio in my MP3 player on in my personal computer. MP3 files are condensed and take up a lot less room in your computer or on a Web site, disc, drive, or other format than an audio .wav file.

For people who are creating "celebration of life" oral or personal history audio tapes, it works well especially for those who prefer not to read their own writing aloud to a tape recorder. Although most people would like to hear their relatives' voices on tape in audio and video, some people are not able to read their works aloud to a recorder or camcorder.

 The synthetic voices will turn any type of writing saved on a disk as a text file into recorded voice—from short poetry to long-length books. The voices are usually recorded with Total Recorder software and saved as an

MP3 file so they can be played on MP3 players or on most computers with CD players.

For those taping persons live in video to make time capsules or other keepsake albums in voice and/or video, it's best to let people think what they are going to say by handing them a list of a few questions. If you're working with a group of older adults, let one of the group members interview another group member by asking each question from a list of several questions.

If you give someone a week's notice to come up with an answer to each question from a list of ten questions and give them two minutes to respond to each question by discussing how it relates to events in their lives or their experiences, you have a twenty minute video tape.

If you allow only a minute for each question from a list of thirty questions, you have a thirty-minute tape. Times may not be exact as people tend to elaborate to flesh out a question. Let the interview and interviewee practice before recording. So it's good to pair up two people. One will ask the interview questions, and the other will answer, talking about turning points and significant events in their lives.

They can be asked whether they have a personal proverb or slogan they live by or a motto or personal logo. Tapes can be anywhere from a half hour to an hour for life stories that can be saved as an MP3 file to a CD. Other files such as a Wave file (.wav) take up too much space on a CD. So they could be condensed into an MP3 file and saved that way. TextAloud and Total Recorder are software programs that save audio files. You can also use Music Match to convert .wav files to MP3 files.

I use TextAloud software and Total Recorder. Also I save the files as MP3 files for an audio CD that will also go up on a Web site. I use Windows Media Player to play the video files and save them as a Windows Media file (WMV file) so they can be easily uploaded to a Web site and still play in Windows Media Player that comes with Windows XP software.

When making time capsules in multimedia, I save on a CD and/or a DVD, and upload the file from my hard disk to a Web site. Copies of the CDs can be given to relatives, the interviewee, museums, libraries, and various schools who may be interested in oral history with a theme.

The themes can be celebrations of life, living time capsules, or fit into any group theme under an umbrella title that holds them together. This can be an era, such as living memories of a particular decade, life experiences in oral history of an area in geography, an ethnic group, or any other heading. Or the tapes can be of individuals or family groups.

Not only life stories, but poetry, plays, novels, stories, and any other form of creative nonfiction or fiction writing can be recorded by synthetic voices as audio story or book collections. Some work well as children's stories and other types of writings as life stories or poetry.

Themes can vary from keepsake albums to time capsules to collections of turning points in history from the life stories of individuals. Also, themes can be recorded as "old time radio" programs or as oral military history from the experiences of veterans and notated to the Veterans History Project at the Library of Congress or other groups and museums.

Make sure you have signed release forms that also release you from liability should any problems arise from putting someone's life story and name on the Web and/or donating it to a library or other public archive.

A good example of a release form is the one posted at the **Veteran's History Project** Web site where life stories of veterans are donated to the Library of Congress and accessible to the public for educational or scholarly research. Check out the .PDF release forms for both the interviewer and the interviewee at their Web site. The **release form** for veterans is at: http://www.loc.gov/folklife/vets/vetform-vetrelease.pdf.

#

Chapter Seven:

 Before Video Recording Life Stories of Older Adults: Questions to Ask

Interviewing for Writing Plays and Skits from Life Stories for Junior and Senior High-School Students and/or Mature Adults.

 STEP 1: Send someone enthusiastic about personal and oral history to senior community centers, lifelong learning programs at universities, nursing homes, or senior apartment complexes activity rooms. You can reach out to a wide variety of older adults in many settings, including at libraries, church groups, hobby and professional or trade associations, unions, retirement resorts, public transportation centers, malls, museums, art galleries, genealogy clubs, and intergenerational social centers.

STEP 2: Have each personal historian or volunteer bring a tape recorder with tape and a note pad. Bring camcorders for recording video to turn into time capsules and CDs or DVDs with life stories, personal history experiences, memoirs, and events highlighting turning points or special times in people's lives.

STEP 3: Assign each personal historian one or two older persons to interview with the following questions.

1. What were the most significant turning points or events in your life?

2. How did you survive the Wars?

3. What were the highlights, turning points, or significant events that you experienced during the economic downturn of 1929-1939? How did you cope or solve your problems?

4. What did you do to solve your problems during the significant stages of your life at age 10, 20, 30, 40, 50, 60 and 70-plus? Or pick a year that you want to talk about.

5. What changes in your life do you want to remember and pass on to future generations?

6. What was the highlight of your life?

7. How is it best to live your life after 70 or 80+?

8. What years do you remember most?

9. What was your favorite stage of life?

10. What would you like people to remember about you and the times you lived through?

STEP 4: Have the student record the older person's answers. Select the most significant events, experiences, or turning points the person chooses to emphasize. Then write the story of that significant event in ten pages or less.

STEP 5: Ask the older person to supply the younger student photos, art work, audio tapes, or video clips. Usually photos, pressed flowers, or art work will be supplied. Have the student or teacher scan the photos onto a disk and return the original photos or art work or music to the owner.

STEP 6: The personal historian, volunteer, student and/or teacher scans the photos and puts them onto a Web site on the Internet at one of the free communities that give away Web site to the public at no cost. Most search engines will give a list of communities at offering free Web sites to the public.

For larger Web site spaces with room for audio and video material and other keepsake memorabilia, purchase a personal Web site from a Web-hosting company or for smaller spaces for photos in a cloud online, research what your computer's or other device's operating system offers, such as space for photo albums in a cloud or space for photos for a limited time. Shop around for affordable Web site space for a ***multimedia life story time capsule*** that would include ***text, video and/or audio clips, music, art, photos,*** and any other effects.

1. Create a Web site with text from the older person's significant life events

2. Add photos.

3. Add audio or video files with the voice and/or images of the older person speaking in small clips or sound bites.

4. Intersperse text and photos or art work with sound, if available.

Add video clips, if available and won't take too much bandwidth.

5. Put Web site on line as **TIME CAPSULE** of (insert name of person) interviewed and edited

by, insert name of student who interviewed
older person.

STEP 7: Label each Web site Time Capsule and
collect them in a history archives on the lives of
older adults at the turn of the millennium.
Make sure the older person and all relatives and
friends are emailed the Web site link. You have
now created a time capsule for future
generations.

**These steps may be used as classroom
exercises at various age or grade levels from
elementary schools to senior community and
lifelong learning centers to teach the following
skills in addition to reminiscing, writing, or
storytelling as a project or as part of a therapy
plan:**

1.   Making friends with older adults.

2.   Learning to write on intergenerational
topics.

3.   Bringing community together of all
generations.

4.   Learning about foster grandparents.

5.   History lessons from those who lived
through history.

6.   Learning about diversity and how people of diverse origins lived through the 20th century.

7.   Preserving the significant events in the lives of people as time capsules for future generations to know what it was like to live between 1900 and 2000 at any age.

8.   Learning to write skits and plays from the life stories of older adults taken down by young students.

9.   Teaching older adults skills in creative writing at senior centers.

10.   Learning what grandma did during World War 2 or the stock market crash of 1929 followed by the economic downturn of 1930-1938.

What to Ask People about Their Lives before You Write a Play or Skit

Step 8: When you interview, ask for facts and concrete details. Look for statistics, and research whether statistics are deceptive in your case.

Step 9: To write a plan, write one sentence for each topic that moves the story or piece forward. Then summarize for each topic in a paragraph. Use dialogue at least in every third paragraph.

Step 10: Look for the following facts or headings to organize your plan for a biography or life story.

1. **PROVERB.** Ask the people you interview what would be their proverb or slogan if they had to create/invent a slogan that fit themselves or their aspirations: One slogan might be something like the seventies ad for cigarettes, "We've come a long way, baby," to signify ambition. Only look for an original slogan.

2. **PURPOSE.** Ask the people you interview or a biography, for what purpose is or was their journey? Is or was it equality in the workplace or something personal and different such as dealing with change--downsizing, working after retirement, or anything else?

3. **IMPRINT.** Ask what makes an imprint or impact on people's lives and what impact the people you're interviewing want to make on others?

4. **STATISTICS:** How deceptive are they? How can you use them to focus on reality?

5. **CHANGES:** How have the people that you're interviewing influenced changes in the way people or corporations function?

6. **GOALS:** To what is the person aspiring?

7. **COMMUNICATION:** What kind of communication skills does the person have and how are these skills received? Are the communication skills male or female, thinking or feeling, yin or yang, soft or steeled, and are people around these people negative or positive about those communication skills?

8. **STYLES:** What new styles is the person using? What kind of motivational methods, structure, or leadership? Is the person a follower or leader? How does the person match his or her personality to the character of a corporation or interest?

9. **CHANGE**: How does the person handle change?

10. **REINFORCEMENTS:** How is the person reinforced?

Once you have titles and summarized paragraphs for each segment of your story, you can more easily flesh out the story by adding dialogue and description to your factual information. Look for differences in style between the people you interview? How does the person want to be remembered?

Is the person a risk taker or cautious for survival? Does the person identify with her job or the people involved in the process of doing the work most creatively or originally?

Does creative expression take precedence over processes of getting work out to the right place at the right time? Does the person want his ashes to spell the words "re-invent yourself" where the sea meets the shore? This is a popular concept appearing in various media.

You May Wish to Search the Records in the Family History Library of Salt Lake City, Utah

Make use of the database online at the Family History Library of Salt Lake City, Utah. Or visit the branches in many locations. The Family History Library (FHL) is known worldwide as the focal point of family history records preservation.

The FHL collection contains more than 2.2 million rolls of microfilmed genealogical records, 742,000 microfiche, 300,000 books, and 4,500 periodicals that represent data collected from over 105 countries. You don't have to be a member of any particular church or faith to use the library or to go online and search the records.

Family history records owe a lot to the invention of writing. And then there is oral history, but someone needs to transcribe oral history to record and archive them for the future.

Interestingly, isn't it a coincidence that writing is 6,000 years old and DNA that existed 6,000 years ago first reached such crowded conditions in the very cities that had first used writing extensively to measure accounting and trade had very little recourse but to move on to new areas where there were far less people and less use of writing?

A lot of major turning points occurred 6,000 years ago--the switch to a grain-based diet from a meat and root diet, the use of bread and fermented grain beverages, making of oil from plants, and the rise of religions based on building "god houses" in the centers of town in areas known as the "cereal belt" around the world.

Six thousand years ago in India we have the start of the Sanskrit writings, the cultivation of grain. In China, we have the recording of acupuncture points for medicine built on energy meridians that also show up in the blue tattoos of the Ice Man fossil "Otsi" in the Alps--along the same meridians as the Chinese acupuncture points.

At 6,000 years ago the Indo European languages spread out across Europe. Mass migrations expanded by the Danube leaving pottery along the trade routes that correspond to the clines and gradients of gene frequency coming out of the cereal belts.

Then something happened. There was an agricultural frontier cutting off the agriculturists from the hunters. Isn't it a coincidence that the agricultural frontiers or barriers also are genetic barriers at least to some degree?

Oral History

Here's how to systematically collect, record, and preserve living peoples' testimonies about their own experiences. After you record in audio and/or video the highlights of anyone's experiences, try to verify your findings. See whether you can check any facts in order to find out whether the person being recorded is making up the story or whether it really did happen.

This is going to be difficult unless you have witnesses or other historical records. Once you have verified your findings to the best of your ability, note whether the findings have been verified. Then analyze what you found. Put the oral history recordings in an accurate historical context.

Mark the recordings with the dates and places. Watch where you store your findings so scholars in the future will be able to access the transcript or recording and convert the recording to another, newer technology. For instance, if you have a transcript on paper, have it saved digitally on a disk and somewhere else on tape and perhaps a written transcript on acid-free good paper in case technology moves ahead before the transcript or recording is converted to the new technology.

 For example, if you only put your recording on a phonograph record, within a generation or two, there may not be any phonographs around to play the record. The same goes for CDs, DVDs and audio or video tapes.

So make sure you have a readable paper copy to be transcribed or scanned into the new technology as well as the recordings on disk and tape. For example, if you record someone's experiences in a live interview with your video camera, use a cable to save the video in the hard disk of a computer and then burn the file to a CD or DVD.

 Keep a copy of audio tape and a copy of regular video tape—all in a safe place such as a time capsule, and make a copy for various archives in libraries and university oral history preservation centers. Be sure scholars in the future can find a way to enjoy the experiences in your time capsule, scrapbook, or other storage device for oral histories.

Use your DNA testing results to add more information to a historical record. As an interviewer with a video camera and/or audio tape recorder, your task is to record as a historical record what the person who you are interviewing recollects.

The events move from the person being interviewed to you, the interviewer, and then into various historical records. In this way you can combine results of DNA testing with actual memories of events. If it's possible, also take notes or have someone take notes in case the tape doesn't pick up sounds clearly.

I had the experience of having a video camera battery go out in spite of all precautions when I was interviewing someone, and only the audio worked. So keep a backup battery on hand whether you use a tape recorder or a video camera. If at all possible, have a partner bring a spare camera and newly recharged battery. A fully charged battery left overnight has a good chance of going out when you need it.

Writing Plays, Skits, or Life Story Highlights from Oral History Transcripts?

Universal values throughout most of history include commitment to family, faith, and work along with some types of achievement to acquire survival skills. To create readers' and media attention to an oral history, it should have some redemptive value to a universal audience. That's the most important point. Make your oral history simple and earthy. Write about real people who have values, morals, and a faith in something greater than themselves that is equally valuable to readers or viewers.

Publishers who buy an oral history written as a book on its buzz value are buying simplicity. It is simplicity that sells and nothing else but simplicity. This is true for oral histories, instructional materials, and fiction. It's good storytelling to say it simply.

Simplicity means the oral history or memoirs book or story gives you all the answers you were looking for in your life in exotic places, but found it close by. What's the great proverb that your oral history is telling the world?

Is it to stand on your own two feet and put bread on your own table for your family? That's the moral point, to pull your own weight, and pulling your own weight is a buzz word that sells oral histories and fiction that won't preach, but instead teach and reach through simplicity.

That's the backbone of the oral historian's new media. Buzz means the story is simple to understand. You make the complex easier to grasp. And buzz means you can sell your story or book, script or narrative by focusing on the values of simplicity, morals, faith, and universal values that hold true for everyone.

Doing the best to take care of your family sells and is buzz appeal, hot stuff in the publishing market of today and in the oral history archives. This is true, regardless of genre. Publishers go through fads every two years--angel books, managing techniques books, computer home-based business books, novels about ancient historical characters or tribes, science fiction, children's programming, biography, and oral history transcribed into a book or play.

The genres shift emphasis, but values are consistent in the bestselling books. Perhaps your oral history will be simple enough to become a bestselling book or script. In the new media, simplicity is buzz along with values.

Oral history, like best-selling novels and true stories is built on simplicity, values, morals, and commitment. Include how one person dealt with about trends. Focus your own oral history about life in the lane of your choice. Develop one central issue and divide that issue into a few important questions that highlight or focus on that one central issue.

When you write or speak a personal history either alone or in an interview, you focus on determining the order of your life story. Don't use flashbacks. Focus on the highlights and turning points. Organize what you'll say or write. An autobiography deals in people's relationships. Your autobiography deals as much with what doesn't change--the essentials--as what life changes you and those around you go through.

Your autobiography should be more concrete than abstract. You want the majority of people to understand what you mean. Say what you mean, and mean what you say. More people understand concrete details than understand abstract ideas.

Be personal in a life story. The more personal you are, the more eternal is your life story. More people will view or read it again and again far into the future. You can emphasize your life's journey and look at the world through your own eyes. To make the structure salable, 'meander' your life as you would travel on a journey. Perhaps you're a winding river meandering around obstacles and competitors. At each stop, you learn your own capabilities and your own place in the world.

The more you meander, the more you take away the urgency from your story that sets up tension in the audience and keeps them on the edge of their seat. Don't let the meandering overpower your sense of urgency. Don't dwell on your reaction. Focus on your action to people and situations. Stay active in your own personal history. In other words, don't repeat how you reacted, but show how you acted.

 Before you sit down to write your autobiography, think of yourself in terms of going on a journey inside the privacy of your purse or wallet. May your purse is the only place where you really do have any privacy. Come up for air when you have hit bottom. Bob up to the sunshine, completely changed or at least matured.

If you have really grown, you will not be blinded by the 'light,' in the figurative sense of enlightenment, as the song goes. Instead, the light (knowledge and/or wisdom) offers insight. So now you have vision along with some hindsight. The next step is learning how to promote and market your salable personal history or life story. Your goal might be foresight, insight, and hindsight.

A biography reports the selected events of another person's life--usually 12 major events in the six various significant events also known as "turning points" and also known as "transition points" of life that would include the highlights of significant events for each of the six stages of growth: 1) infanthood, 2) childhood, 3) teen years 4) young adulthood 5) middle life 6) maturity.

#

Chapter Eight:

Life Story Plays as Dialogues with the Higher Self

 If your autobiography has punch and power, is marketable and makes viewers want to network and discuss it in quality circles, your life story will make a concrete impact on the abstract idea of diary writing. Some pause to write from introspection and reflection.

Others prefer to write action from biography. Your mission, should you decide to broadcast it, is to locate business people who want to buy or sell a true life story. It's as profitable for them as it's a healing experience for you if you see it as an exercise in getting to know yourself. Writing and recording your personal history is a search for your core identity.

Personal history writing and speaking or recording reminds me of Stan Dale's quote, "Intimacy is spelled "in to me you see." The quote also is listed on the New Intimacy Web site at http://www.menstuff.org/columns/newintimacy/52.html.

Writing personal history is writing about intimacy. An autobiography helps you practice seeing another person with your soul. Writing the life story as a play, skit, or monologue for high-school performers or older adults offers you a vitality. In the writing process, you see who you are and make a connection with others who shaped your world as you, in turn, shaped the world of those around you.

When you write your autobiography, listen with your body. One of the conclusions many autobiography writers arrive at is "I am never enough." This decision isn't commercial, although the story line with an upbeat ending is marketable. The "not enough" feeling you write in your diary creates fear and loneliness.

What would happen if you took a plot line of a protagonist who says: "I'm not enough or give me a break" and linked it with an antagonist who says: "I need a connection." You have opposites, perhaps a couple. One says, "I need a break." The other replies, "Not until I have a connection."

Then your power-punch your one-liner in the dialogue. "Give me a break" could mask profound loneliness with a tough outer shell (as in I don't need anybody). Your antagonist might continue with a response that repeated "Not without a connection."

The dialogue would be between two people who want a relationship so eagerly that one of them could be more willing to openly work lovingly for it. Your premise would be that the protagonist is really saying, "I don't know how to connect."

The audience sees the deep suffering and the false armor in dialogue and visual action. Not everyone wants other people in a personal history. Do you really want you and your competition in your personal history video? Not unless you're making a feature film about your life.

In reality, you can sell your life story to a small press publisher, to an independent, low-budget producer, or produce it as a play for a few thousand dollars in a local theatre. What else can you expect? That all depends on how commercial your story is written in the eyes of the big studios.

The least expensive way to handle a personal history is to put it on a DVD and on a CD. Have a text copy, and if you have a Web site, upload the video clip and text to the Web as a time capsule. Designate someone to take over the payments on the Web site when you can no longer maintain it. You can even rent an option to someone else's life story's movie rights.

If you want power over your life story, look at the structure of your personal history. If you know you have a salable story, how many ways can you market your autobiographical or biographical writing?

One way to market your story is by utilizing interactive computer software to help yourself and others to write their own life events document. There are several computer software disks on the market that will organize your life story events.

You can form quality circles and teach life story writing to groups, including adult education classes and at senior community centers. Plays are in demand for children, junior high, high school, and college-age performers and audiences as well as performers and audiences of mature adults/senior citizens at their community centers and lifelong learning programs.

Will Computer Software Help You Write Your Life Story?

You may first wish to market your autobiography on computer software disks. Interactive fiction is a writing game recorded on a computer floppy disk which allows the player to answer questions, but the easiest way is to put your video on a flash drive, DVD, or online at a site that lets you upload your video, text, imagery, photo, and audio files.

There are alternative answers. This game is suitable for playing "What if I chose the road not taken? What would my life story be like, then?" To create and market an interactive fiction autobiography game, hire an independent programmer who specializes in programming floppy disk software with questions and alternative answers.

Turn a keepsake album into a skit for a time capsule. Put your life story on the Web or on a DVD and CD at the same time you publish it as a book. Self-publishing will give you the electronic and audio rights to your book. With print-on-demand publishing, you lose your electronic rights in many cases. Check out your contract.

If you go the way of complicated interactive story writing, you'll need to work with someone who knows how to create interactive stories. When a player is interactive, it means he/she interacts with the computer in a learning situation.

For example, the computer software could be designed to ask you these following questions: "What if you chose to become a paralegal instead of a full-time freelance writer? Would freelance writers have the starving artist mentality? What if your fiction always has been rejected? What if you are totally dependent on relatives for support? Where would you be working today?

Would you be happy? How much would you be earning? Who would you meet and marry? Would he/she be kind or abusive? Would you be a co-dependent seeking to be parented?

Interactive software allows you to play the possibilities or create new realities in the present. You can team up with a programmer. Another alternative is using strictly autobiographical software to organize your life story like a diary. You can look back on the result and judge whether it is commercial or strictly for the family genealogy collection.

You may wish to use software to organize your own life story and print out a document. Some story organizing software breaks your history into manageable sections. In fact, some story writing software offer more than 400 specific questions to prompt you to provide details of each area of your life. If you use this type of software, you answer by keyboarding in all the important details into your computer. Then you save it on a disk for posterity. Answer only the questions you choose.

The programs work by advancing one screen at a time when you feel like it. You can spend years writing your autobiography or just a few days. The programs include topics such as your birth, medical events, friends, education, property, holidays, achievements, and other categories. These types of story writing programs might organize various categories and the facts in them so you can glance at your life and decide whether to turn it into a novel, a screenplay, a stage play, video, radio play, audio, or leave it as a book for the family eyes only.

When you're finished typing in the details of each event, you can print your story or export the file to your word processing program or desktop publishing software for formatting into a small tale or a full document. Some of these programs allow you to write a large number of pages, even up to 3,000 pages.

You can print out the document and have it bound in a cover by a photocopying company. Then present it to each family member as a holiday gift. You can use this document to set the record straight, to write your memoirs, or to create every detail of your life or anyone else's life for relatives or for history.

Long after you're gone, your descendants will read it. You can even explain why you included or excluded certain relatives out of your will.

You can pass on information about your marriage to your children so they would repeat or avoid the same choices based on the events of your early childhood programming or whatever you choose to detail. Public domain software offers various programs on creating diaries and life events on software. For other types of software consult software catalogues, public domain software listings, computer bulletin boards and trade journals.

Software can be used two ways: 1: To sell your own autobiography interactive games or 2: To organize and print out your own life events by answering interactive questions on already existing autobiography-writing software. Desktop video combines computer software, burning files to DVD, flash drive, and/or uploading to an online site, and transferring video recordings to other more permanent drives, discs, or other devices as technology changes. Transcribe audio or video recordings for time capsules. You can save the transcripts on parchment or other long-lasting pages to be read far in the future. Sometimes desktop publishing combines with desktop video also known as multimedia authoring.

You may choose to create video programs that can be used interactively with computer software to ask someone hundreds of questions about autobiographical events. I like putting material on CDs or DVDs and mailing them to my online students when I used to teach university-level writing and speaking courses entirely online.

If you're a facilitator, you can help others to write, illustrate or to express themselves in multimedia. Writing personal histories interactively with video and computers works very well with senior citizens taking an autobiography writing class in a community center.

Psychotherapists will also find this introspective way of writing works well with clients who would rather share their innermost thoughts and details of life events with a computer. To protect the privacy of people, it's a good way of "getting thoughts and feelings off your chest in words.

 When you go public, ask yourself how your researched information can be of help to others who seek your information for making choices and decisions in their own lives. Personal history writing also helps you seek self-identity and share your introspective feelings on paper or through interviews on video or audio without direct contact with a group. You can dialogue with the questions on the computer in total privacy.

\#

Chapter Nine:

Offering Life Stories to Audiences Storytelling and/or Writing

Launch your salable life story in the major national press and in various newspapers and magazines of niche markets related to the events in your life, such as weekly newspapers catering to a group: senior citizens, your ethnic group, your local area, or your occupation or area of interest. Your personal history time capsule may be saved to disk and also uploaded to the Web. What about looking for movie deals and book publishers?

If you don't have the money to produce your autobiography as a video biography, or even a film or commercial movie, or publish it for far less cost as a print-on-demand published book, you may wish to find a co-production partner to finance the production of your life story as a cinematic film or made-for-TV video.

At the same time you could contact literary agents and publishers, but one front-page article in a national newspaper or daily newspaper can do wonders to move your life story in front of the gaze of publishers and producers. While you're waiting for a reporter to pay attention to the news angle you have selected for your life story, I highly recommend Michael Wiese's book Film and Video Marketing because it lists some co-production partners as the following:

Private Investors/Consortiums

Foreign Governments (blocked funds)

Financiers

Corporations

Theatrical Distributors

International Theatrical Distributors

International Sales Agents

Home Video

International Home Video

Pay TV

Syndicators

Record Companies

Music Publishers

Book Publishers

Toy Companies

Licensing and Merchandising Firms

Sponsors (products, services)

Public Relations Firms

Marketing Companies/Consultants

Film Bookers

You can also contact actors, directors, producers, feature distributors, home video distributors, entertainment lawyers, brokers, accountants, animation houses, production houses, video post-production houses, labs, film facilities, and agents with your script and ask the owners whether they'd be interested in bartering budget items, deferring, or investing in your script.

Private investors could also be professional investors, venture capitalists, and even doctors and dentists who may wish to finance a movie if the potential interests them. You can sell points in your film to investors who finance it as a group of investors, each buying a small percentage of the film for an investment fee.

Or you can approach film investment corporations that specialize in investing in and producing films as partners. They are publicized or listed in the entertainment trade magazines going to producers and workers in the entertainment and film or video industry.

You market your script not only to agents and producers, but to feature distributors, film financiers and co-production partners. This is the first step in finding a way to take your autobiography from script to screen. Learn who distributes what before you approach anyone.

If you want to approach video instead of film, you might wish to know that children's video programming is the fastest-growing genre in original programming. Children's titles account for 10%-15% of the overall home video revenues.

According to one of Michael Wiese's books written in the nineties, Home Video: Producing for the Home Market, "With retail prices falling and alternative retail outlets expanding, children's programming will soon become one of the most profitable segments of the video market." He was right. What has happened in the new millennium is that children's program is doing wonderfully.

Why? Children's video is repeatable. Children watch the same tape 30 to 50 times. Children's video sells for comparatively lower prices than feature films.

Children's video also rents well. Children's tapes sell it toy stores, book stores, children's stores, and in stores like Woolworth's and Child World. Manufacturers sell tapes at Toy Fair and the American Booksellers Association conventions. For these reasons, you may wish to write your autobiography as a script for children's video or as a children's book. Video is a burgeoning industry.

According to the market research firm, Fairfield Group, in 1985, the prerecorded video business earned $ 3.3 billion in sales and rentals. This nearly equaled the record and theatrical box office revenues for the same year. The world VCR population is about 100 million. Today we have the DVD and the Internet streaming video.

Back in 1985, the U.S. and Japan accounted for half of the VCRs, followed by the United Kingdom, (9 million) West Germany (nearly 7 million), and Canada, Australia, Turkey, and France (about 3 million each). Spain reported 2 million VCRs. By 1991, the number of VCR ownership increased as prices slowly came down.

Today, in the 21st century, the prerecorded video business has quickly moved to DVD disks, downloadable at a price Internet-based movies, and video tapes are on the way to being a memory of the eighties and early nineties. In the next decade, another media format will be in fashion to replace videos on DVDs and streaming Internet video. The idea is to keep transferring the story from one form of technology to another so that videos made today will be able to be viewed by people in the next century.

The European VCR markets grew faster than in the U.S. during the eighties and nineties just as the DVD markets grew in the early 21st century because there were fewer entertainment alternatives--fewer TV stations, restricted viewing hours, fewer pay TV services, and fewer movie theatres.

You should not overlook the foreign producers for your script. Include Canadian cable T.V., foreign agents, and foreign feature film and video producers among your contacts. Most university libraries open to the public for research include directories listing foreign producers.

Photocopy their addresses and send them a query letter and one-page synopsis of your script. Don't overlook the producers from non-English speaking countries. Your script can be translated or dubbed.

You might attend film market type conventions and conferences. They draw producers from a variety of countries. In 1989 at the former Cinetex Film Market in Las Vegas, producers from Canada, Italy, Israel, Spain, and other foreign countries sat next to script writers. All of them were receptive to receiving scripts. They handed one another their business cards. You can learn a lot at summer film markets and film festivals about what kind of scripts are in demand.

Keep a list of which film markets will meet. In the U.S. there are 3 to 5 film markets a year and many more film festivals. Seek out the foreign and local producers with track records and see whether they'd be interested in your script if you have a life story in the form of a script, treatment, or story.

Perhaps your theme has some relation to a producer's country or ethnic group. Lots of films are made in East and South Asia, in the Middle East (Israel, Egypt and Tunisia), in Latin America, Malaysia, Europe, and Canada.

Seek out the Australian producers also and New Zealand or India. If you have a low-budget film or home video script set in Korea, Philippines, Japan, or Taiwan, or a specialty film such as Karate or something that appeals to the Indian film market, contact those producers and script agents in those countries. Find out the budget limitations that producers have in the different countries.

Social issues documentaries based on your autobiography are another market for home video. Vestron and other home video distributors use hard-hitting documentaries. Collecting documentary video tapes is like collecting copies of National Geographic magazine. You never throw them out. Tapes are also sold by direct mail. Companies producing and distributing documentaries include MCA, MGM/UA, Vestron, Victory, CBS/Fox, Warner, Media, Karl, Monterey, Thorn/EMI, Embassy, and USA, to name a few.

If you write your autobiography or another's biography as a romance, you might wish to write a script for the video romance series market. Romance video has its roots in the paperback novel. However, the biggest publishers of romance novels have little recognition in retail video stores.

Among consumers, yes; wholesalers and retailers, no. Bookstores, yes. The problem is with pricing. To sell romance videos in bookstores, the DVDs or other medium for video and audio would have to be sold at less than $29. History has shown what has happened to video stores popular in the 1980s now that streaming video or discs and pay TV has changed how people buy or rent movies to watch at home.

Nowadays, instead of people going to video stores to rent DVDs to see movies, they can stream the movie, buy the movie to download, or go to most supermarket vending machines to rent DVDs that contain popular movies and animation for various age levels of viewers. Technology is constantly changing in the way video is rented.

Yet you still can't find a supermarket vending machine with recorded videos to rent of people's life stories. That's still for the time capsules for future generations to review the life and times of family members, friends, and acquaintances of past generations.

Production costs to make high quality romance videos are high. Top stars, top writers, hit book titles, exotic locations, music and special effects are required. Huge volumes of tapes must be sold to break even. Then producers have to search for pay TV, broadcast, or foreign partners. The budget for a one-hour video tape of a thin romance story comes to $500,000.

It's far better to make a low-budget feature film. Romance as a genre has never previously appealed to the video retail buyer. In contrast, a romance paperback sells for a few dollars. Now the question remains: Would women buy a romance-genre video DVD priced at $9.95?

Romance novels successfully have been adapted to audio tape for listening at far less than the cost of video. There is a market for audio scripts of short romance novels and novellas. What is becoming popular today are videos and 'movies' downloadable from the Internet that you can watch on your computer screen or save to a DVD since DVD burners became affordable and popular. Try adapting highlights of your romance or life story novel to a play, skit, or monologue.

The only way romance videos would work is by putting together a multi-partnered structure that combines pay TV, home video, book publishing, and domestic and foreign TV. Several decades ago, in the 1980s, was anyone doing romance video tapes before DVDs were readily available with movies people could rent or purchase? Yes. Prism Video back then produced six feature-length romance films, acquired from Comworld. In 1985 the tapes sold for $11.95.

Comworld had limited TV syndication exposure and was one of the first to come out with romance videos. Karl/Lorimar came out with eight romance films from L/A House Productions on a budget of $400,000 each. They were also priced at $11.95 in 1985. To break even, a company has to sell about 60,000 units per title.

Twenty years later, think about adapting to a play the romance DVD video and the downloadable Internet video. What's available to adapt as educational material? Write for various age groups on niche subjects that would appeal to teachers. Follow their rules on what is appropriate for their classrooms. The market also is open for stage and radio/Internet broadcast skits and plays geared to older adults as performers and audiences.

Other media are like open doors to finding a way to put your life story on a disk. Any interview, script, or story can go from print-on-demand published novel or true story book to radio script or stage play. A video several decades ago could move from a digital high 8 camcorder with a Firewire 1394 cable attached to a personal computer rapidly into the hard disk drive via Windows XP Movie Maker software.

From there it would have been saved as a WMV file (a Windows Media file). Then the file would have been recorded at home on a DVD, if long, or a CD if under one hour. Just like in the past decades, nowadays, poems still can be written, read, and 'burned' to a compact disk or DVD or flash drive/thumb drive, or other device, and then mailed out as greeting cards, love letters, or personal histories. Short videos can be emailed. Or the same nowadays can be downloaded from an online site.

Romance or life story highlights novels and scripts on audio tape cost less to produce. This market occasionally advertises for romantic novel manuscripts, scripts, and stories in a variety of writer's magazines. Check out the needs of various magazines for journalists and writers online. If you read a lot of romance genre novels or write in this style, you may want to write your autobiography in this genre, but you'd have to market to publishers who use this genre or biographies in other genres such as factual biography.

If your autobiography is set on events which occurred in your childhood, you might prefer to concentrate on writing appropriate for children's video programming. It's a lot easier to sell to the producers who are basking in the current explosion of children's video programming. Perhaps it's your mission to use the video format to teach children.

Will the script of your life story do the following?

Teach,

Mentor,

Motivate,

Inspire,

Or inform viewers who can be:

Children,

Teenagers,

Parents

Or 'midlifers' and senior citizens on their quests for self-identify:

Or in their search for facts:

To use as guidelines in making their own decisions:

About life's journeys and writing an introspective journal?

Can your diary be dynamic, dramatic, and empowering to others who may be going through similar stages of life? Are your characters charismatic and memorable, likable and strong?

A life story or autobiography when videotaped or filed as a feature-length movie can spring out of a diary or an inner personal journal (which dialogues with the people who impact your life and observes selected, important events).

#

Chapter Ten:

Stories with Central Issues

Plays, Skits, or Stories with Current Events or Social History:

Diaries, like deleted files hidden in the cache pits of computers, and DNA tests can be used as evidence. Diaries also hold the seeds of a story. You could write a novel or a screenplay from a diary. A diary also is a history.

Preserve a diary as you would restore and preserve a valuable work of art from the past. Diaries are meant to be passed to future generations for a glimpse into a world that can be experienced by generations far into the future. Keep a file of dates listed in the diary and any objects that surrounded the diary from the same era.

A story with a central issue needed little explanation when one woman wrote in her diary in the style of a telegram: "October 25, 1926: First day of honeymoon. On train to Miami. Today I died." What central issues and themes tell a story in the diaries that cross your path?

Instead of writing about pain, write to cheer people up with nourishment. That's why nourishment-for-the-soul-themed books are popular. People want to be cheered up, not always read your painful experiences.

Write so people will feel important about themselves, feel good, positive, and nourished from how you solved your problems or gained results. Write about current events, social history and issues, or real life experiences that transformed you. People read or watch a play also for information they can use in making decisions and choices.

It's not always escape or distraction from real life, but nourishment and solutions to problems that offer action, closure, and hope. Plays that offer harmony and serenity as escape and distraction also form part of the plays and skits of nourishment skits. Don't always give them pain to read. It's therapeutic for you, but not as a steady diet for your audiences.

They already watch the news on TV. How can you transcend and transform the news as nourishment and reality, and still sell escape? Keep the dates and topics organized if you are working with restoring and preserving diaries and turning them into skits and plays for various age groups.

There should be a central issue or theme. How old was the person writing the diary? How many years did the individual keep the diary? What kind of objects were near the diary, packed together?

What kind of dust or other stains were on the diary—sawdust? Farm materials and plants? The first corsage from the senior prom? How about recipes, household hints, or how-to tips for hobbies? Was the diary or journal personal and inner-reflected, or geared toward outer events in the world? Were anecdotes about people and/or pets included, or was it about the feelings of the author of the diary?

Find out what other clues the mystery of the diary unfolds, from the lipstick or nail polish stain to the sawdust and coffee stains, or that faint smell of tobacco, industrial lint, or is it lavender, jasmine or farm dust and straw? Look inside the box in which the diary was packed. It's all evidence and clues waiting to be examined just like a mystery novel. A diary is a story, and everyone life deserves a novel, story, or biography and eventually, a place in a time capsule.

#

Chapter Eleven:

How to Restore, Recover, and Adapt Diaries into Plays or Skits

Make a book jacket for your diary to preserve and restore it. Use acid-free paper. Call a library or museum and ask for a brand or type of long lasting acid-free paper and where you can buy some. Put a title and label on the dust jacket with the name of the diary's author and any dates, city, state, or country.

You can also speak to the art history department of most universities and find out what kind of paper is best to use for a book jacket to restore and preserve a diary. Treat it like a work of art. The same can be done for photo scrap books.

If torn, mend the diary. Your goal is to improve its condition. Apply a protective plastic wrapper to your valuable dust jacket. Give the diary a dust jacket in good condition. It should start to look more like a valuable book in good condition.

If the diary is dingy and dirty, bleach it white on the edges. Put a plastic cover on the diary. The white pages of a diary without ink can be bleached with regular household bleach, but don't let the vapors of the bleach soak through to reach the ink because it will bleach out the writing.

Repair old diaries and turn them into heirlooms for families and valuable collectibles. The current price for repair of handwritten diaries and books is about $35 and up per book or bound diary, if you like to specialize in mending old dairies and family or personal books for a fee.

Some old diaries contain recipes and also served as personal, handwritten cookbooks containing recipes created by a particular family or family cook. These were valuable books preserved as if they were family scrapbooks, unlike the recipe databases in computers we have today. They are works of art, like an old tapestry embroidered with the story of a family's major turning points and events. For more repair tips on bound diaries and books, you may wish to see, *How to Wrap a Book,* Fannie Merit Farmer. Boston Cooking School.

How do you repair an old diary to make it more valuable to the heirs? You'll often find a bound diary that's torn in the seams. In the 1990s, according to Barbara Gelink, of the *Collector's Old Cookbooks Club*, San Diego, whom I interviewed *in the 1990s* for a magazine article, to repair a book, you take a bottle of Book Saver Glue (or any other book-repairing or wood glue), and spread the glue along the binder.

Run the glue along the seam and edges. Use wax paper to keep the glue from getting where it shouldn't. Put a heavy glass bottle on the inside page to hold it down while the glue dries.

To remove tape, tags, or stains from a glossy cover, use lighter fluid or cleaning fluid (away from sparks, flames, or heat lamps). Dampen a cloth with nail polish remover if lighter fluid is too smelly and flammable for you.

Another way to remove something pasted on a plastic book cover is to use the finest grade sandpaper. Many books you'll find at goodwill will have adhesive price tags on the book.

It's not usual to find diaries, even bound diaries in old book stores, but they show up in garage sales and in some antique stores and flea markets along with old photos.

You can design time capsules that will keep memorabilia for the next few generations to open in the time you ask in your request with that time capsule.

#

Chapter Twelve:

Interviewing Techniques for Video biographies: Techniques for Recording Life Stories and Highlights You'll write as Plays, Dramatizations, or Skits - Reminisce therapeutically

The events move from the person being interviewed to you, the interviewer, and then into various historical records. In this way you can combine results of DNA testing with actual memories of events. If it's possible, also take notes or have someone take notes in case the tape doesn't pick up sounds clearly.

Keep a backup battery on hand whether you use a tape recorder or a video camera. If at all possible, have a partner bring a spare camera and newly recharged battery. A fully charged battery left overnight has a good chance of going out when you need it.

What Should Go Into a Life Story Play, Skit, or Dramatization?

Emphasize the commitment to family and faith. To create readers' and media attention to an oral history, it should have some redemptive value to a universal audience. That's the most important point. Make your oral history simple and earthy. Write about real people who have values, morals, and a faith in something greater than themselves that is equally valuable to readers or viewers.

Publishers who buy an oral history written as a book on its buzz value are buying simplicity. It is simplicity that sells and nothing else but simplicity. This is true for oral histories, instructional materials, and fiction. It's good storytelling to say it simply.

Simplicity means the oral history or memoirs book or story gives you all the answers you were looking for in your life in exotic places, but found it close by. What's the great proverb that your oral history is telling the world?

Is it to stand on your own two feet and put bread on your own table for your family? That's the moral point, to pull your own weight, and pulling your own weight is a buzz word that sells oral histories and fiction that won't preach, but instead teach and reach through simplicity.

That's the backbone of the oral historian's new media. Buzz means the story is simple to understand. You make the complex easier to grasp. And buzz means you can sell your story or book, script or narrative by focusing on the values of simplicity, morals, faith, and universal values that hold true for everyone.

 Doing the best to take care of your family sells and is buzz appeal, hot stuff in the publishing market of today and in the oral history archives. This is true, regardless of genre. Publishers go through fads every two years--angel books, managing techniques books, computer home-based business books, novels about ancient historical characters or tribes, science fiction, children's programming, biography, and oral history transcribed into a book or play.

The genres shift emphasis, but values are consistent in the bestselling books. Perhaps your oral history will be simple enough to become a bestselling book or script. In the new media, simplicity is buzz along with values. Oral history, like best-selling novels and true stories is built on simplicity, values, morals, and commitment. Include how one person dealt with about trends. Focus your own oral history about life in the lane of your choice.

#

Chapter Thirteen:

Steps to Take in Gathering Life Story Highlights to Write into Plays or Skits

Use the following sequence when gathering oral/aural histories:

1.   Develop one central issue and divide that issue into a few important questions that highlight or focus on that one central issue.

2.   Write out a plan just like a business plan for your oral history project. You may have to use that plan later to ask for a grant for funding, if required. Make a list of all your products that will result from the oral history when it's done.

3.   Write out a plan for publicity or public relations and media relations. How are you going to get the message to the public or special audiences?

4.   Develop a budget. This is important if you want a grant or to see how much you'll have to spend on creating an oral history project.

5.   List the cost of video recording and editing, packaging, publicity, and help with audio or special effects and stock shot photos of required.

6.   What kind of equipment will you need? List that and the time slots you give to each part of the project. How much time is available? What are your deadlines?

7.   What's your plan for a research? How are you going to approach the people to get the interviews? What questions will you ask?

8.   Do the interviews. Arrive prepared with a list of questions. It's okay to ask the people the kind of questions they would like to be asked. Know what dates the interviews will cover in terms of time. Are you covering the economic depression of the thirties? World Wars? Fifties? Sixties? Pick the time parameters.

9.   Edit the interviews so you get the highlights of experiences and events, the important parts. Make sure what's important to you also is important to the person you interviewed.

10.   Find out what the interviewee wants to emphasize perhaps to highlight events in a life story. Create a video-biography of the highlights of one person's life or an oral history of an event or series of events.

11.   Process audio as well as video, and make sure you have written transcripts of

anything on audio and/or video in case the technology changes or the tapes go bad.

12.   Save the tapes to compact disks, DVDs, a computer hard disk and several other ways to preserve your oral history time capsule. Donate any tapes or CDs to appropriate archives, museums, relatives of the interviewee, and one or more oral history libraries. They are usually found at universities that have an oral history department and library such as UC Berkeley and others.

13.   Check the Web for oral history libraries at universities in various states and abroad.

14.   Evaluate what you have edited. Make sure the central issue and central questions have been covered in the interview. Find out whether newspapers or magazines want summarized transcripts of the audio and/or video with photos.

15.   Contact libraries, archives, university oral history departments and relevant associations and various ethnic genealogy societies that focus on the subject matter of your central topic.

16.   Keep organizing what you have until you have long and short versions of your oral history for various archives and publications.

Contact magazines and newspapers to see whether editors would assign reporters to do a story on the oral history project.

17.   Create a scrapbook with photos and summarized oral histories. Write a synopsis of each oral history on a central topic or issue. Have speakers give public presentations of what you have for each person interviewed and/or for the entire project using highlights of several interviews with the media for publicity. Be sure your project is archived properly and stored in a place devoted to oral history archives and available to researchers and authors.

Aural/Oral History Techniques

1.   Begin with easy to answer questions that don't require you explore and probe deeply in your first question. Focus on one central issue when asking questions. Don't use abstract questions. A plain question would be "What's your purpose?" An abstract question with connotations would be "What's your crusade?" Use questions with denotations instead of connotations. Keep questions short and plain--easy to understand. Examples would be, "What did you want to accomplish? How did you solve those problems? How did you find closure?" Ask the familiar "what, when, who, where, how, and why."

2.   First research written or visual resources before you begin to seek an oral history of a central issue, experience, or event.

3.   Who is your intended audience?

4.   What kind of population niche or sample will you target?

5.   What means will you select to choose who you will interview? What group of people will be central to your interview?

6.   Write down how you'll explain your project. Have a script ready so you don't digress or forget what to say on your feet.

7.   Consult oral history professionals if you need more information. Make sure what you write in your script will be clear to understand by your intended audience.

8.   Have all the equipment you need ready and keep a list of what you'll use and the cost. Work up your budget.

9.   Choose what kind of recording device is best—video, audio, multimedia, photos, and text transcript. Make sure your video is broadcast quality. I use a Sony Digital eight (high eight) camera.

10.   Make sure from cable TV stations or news stations that what type of video and audio you choose ahead of time is broadcast quality.

11.   Make sure you have an external microphone and also a second microphone as a second person also tapes the interview in case the quality of your camera breaks down. You can also keep a tape recorder going to capture the audio in case your battery dies.

12.   Make sure your battery is fully charged right before the interview. Many batteries die down after a day or two of nonuse.

13.   Test all equipment before the interview and before you leave your office or home. I've had batteries go down unexpectedly and happy there was another person ready with another video camera waiting and also an audio tape version going.

14.   Make sure the equipment works if it's raining, hot, cold, or other weather variations. Test it before the interview. Practice interviewing someone on your equipment several times to get the hang of it before you show up at the interview.

15.   Make up your mind how long the interview will go before a break and use tape of that length, so you have one tape for each

segment of the interview. Make several copies of your interview questions.

16.   Make sure the interviewee has a copy of the questions long before the interview so the person can practice answering the questions and think of what to say or even take notes. Keep checking your list of what you need to do.

17.   Let the interviewee make up his own questions if he wants. Perhaps your questions miss the point. Present your questions first. Then let him embellish the questions or change them as he wants to fit the central issue with his own experiences.

18.   Call the person two days and then one day before the interview to make sure the individual will be there on time and understands how to travel to the location. Or if you are going to the person's home, make sure you understand how to get there.

19.   Allow yourself one extra hour in case of traffic jams.

20.   Choose a quiet place. Turn off cell phones and any ringing noises. Make sure you are away from barking dogs, street noise, and other distractions.

21.   Before you interview make sure the person knows he or she is going to be video and audio-taped.

22.   If you don't want anyone swearing, make that clear it's for public archives and perhaps broadcast to families.

23.   Your interview questions should follow the journalist's information-seeking format of asking, who, what, where, where, how, and why. Oral history is a branch of journalistic research.

24.   Let the person talk and don't interrupt. You be the listener and think of oral history as aural history from your perspective.

25.   Make sure only one person speaks without being interrupted before someone else takes his turn to speak.

26.   Understand silent pauses are for thinking of what to say.

27.   Ask one question and let the person gather his thoughts.

28.   Finish all your research on one question before jumping to the next question. Keep it organized by not jumping back to the first question after the second is done. Stay in a linear format.

29.   Follow up what you can about any one question, finish with it, and move on to the next question without circling back. Focus on listening instead of asking rapid fire questions as they would confuse the speaker.

30.   Ask questions that allow the speaker to begin to give a story, anecdote, life experience, or opinion along with facts. Don't ask questions that can be answered only be yes or no. This is not a courtroom. Let the speaker elaborate with facts and feelings or thoughts.

31.   Late in the interview, start to ask questions that explore and probe for deeper answers.

32.   Wrap up with how the person solved the problem, achieved results, reached a conclusion, or developed an attitude, or found the answer. Keep the wrap-up on a light, uplifting note.

33.   Don't leave the individual hanging in emotion after any intensity of. Respect the feelings and opinions of the person. He or she may see the situation from a different point of view than someone else. So respect the person's right to feel as he does. Respect his need to recollect his own experiences.

34.	Interview for only one hour at a time. If you have only one chance, interview for an hour. Take a few minutes break. Then interview for the second hour. Don't interview more than two hours at any one meeting.

35.	Use prompts such as paintings, photos, music, video, diaries, vintage clothing, crafts, antiques, or memorabilia when appropriate. Carry the photos in labeled files or envelopes to show at appropriate times in order to prime the memory of the interviewee.

For example, you may show a childhood photo and ask "What was it like in that orphanage where these pictures were taken?" Or travel photos might suggest a trip to America as a child, or whatever the photo suggests.

You might ask, "Do you remember when this ice cream parlor inside the ABC movie house stood at the corner of X and Y Street? Did you go there as a teenager? What was your funniest memory of this movie theater or the ice cream store inside back in the fifties?"

36.	As soon as the interview is over, label all the tapes and put the numbers in order.

37.	A signed release form is required before you can broadcast anything. So have the interviewee sign a release form before the interview.

38.   Make sure the interviewee gets a copy of the tape and a transcript of what he or she said on tape. If the person insists on making corrections, send the paper transcript of the tape for correction to the interviewee. Edit the tape as best you can or have it edited professionally.

39.   Make sure you comply with all the corrections the interviewee wants changed. He or she may have given inaccurate facts that need to be corrected on the paper transcript.

40.   Have the tape edited with the corrections, even if you have to make a tape at the end of the interviewee putting in the corrections that couldn't be edited out or changed.

41.   As a last resort, have the interviewee redo the part of the tape that needs correction and have it edited in the tape at the correct place marked on the tape. Keep the paper transcript accurate and up to date, signed with a release form by the interviewee.

42.   Oral historians write a journal of field notes about each interview. Make sure these

get saved and archived so they can be read with the transcript.

43.   Have the field notes go into a computer where someone can read them along with the transcript of the oral history video, audio, drive, online site, or disc.

44.   Thank the interviewee in writing for taking the time to do an interview for broadcast and transcript.

45.   Put a label on everything you do from the interview to the field notes. Make a file and sub file folders and have everything stored in a computer, in archived storage, and in paper transcript.

46.   Make copies and digital copies of all photos and put into the records in a computer. Return originals to owners.

47.   Make sure you keep your fingerprints off the photos by wearing white cotton gloves. Use cardboard when sending the photos back and pack securely. Also photocopy the photos and scan the photos into your computer. Treat photos as antique art history in preservation.

48.   Make copies for yourself of all photos, tapes, and transcripts. Use your duplicates, and store the original as the master tape in a place

that won't be used often, such as a time capsule or safe, or return to a library or museum where the original belongs.

49.   Return all original photos to the owners. An oral history archive library or museum also is suitable for original tapes. Use copies only to work from, copy, or distribute.

50.   Index your tapes and transcripts. To use oral history library and museum terminology, recordings and transcripts are given "accession numbers."

51.   Phone a librarian in an oral history library of a university for directions on how to assign accession numbers to your tapes and transcripts if the materials are going to be stored at that particular library. Store copies in separate places in case of loss or damage.

52.   If you don't know where the materials will be stored, use generic accession numbers to label your tapes and transcripts. Always keep copies available for yourself in case you have to duplicate the tapes to send to an institution, museum, or library, or to a broadcast company.

53.   Make synopses available to public broadcasting radio and TV stations.

54.   Check your facts.

55.   Are you missing anything you want to include?

56.   Is there some place you want to send these tapes and transcripts such as an ethnic museum, radio show, or TV satellite station specializing in the topics on the tapes, such as public TV stations? Would it be suitable for a world music station? A documentary station?

57.   If you need more interviews, arrange them if possible.

58.   Give the interviewee a copy of the finished product with the corrections. Make sure the interviewee signs a release form that he or she is satisfied with the corrections and is releasing the tape to you and your project.

59.   Store the tapes and transcripts in a library or museum or at a university or other public place where it will be maintained and preserved for many generations and restored when necessary.

60.   You can also send copies to a film repository or film library that takes video tapes, an archive for radio or audio tapes for radio broadcast or cable TV.

61.   Copies may be sent to various archives for storage that lasts for many generations.

Always ask whether there are facilities for restoring the tape. A museum would most likely have these provisions as would a large library that has an oral history library project or section.

62.   Make sure the master copy is well protected and set up for long-term storage in a place where it will be protected and preserved.

63.   If the oral history is about events in history, various network news TV stations might be interested. Film stock companies may be interested in copies of old photos.

64.   Find out from the subject matter what type of archives, repository, or storage museums and libraries would be interested in receiving copies of the oral history tapes and transcripts.

65.   Print media libraries would be interested in the hard paper copy transcripts and photos as would various ethnic associations and historical preservation societies. Find out whether the materials will go to microfiche, film, or be digitized and put on CDs and DVDs, or on the World Wide Web. If you want to create a time capsule for the Web, you can ask the interviewee whether he or she wants the materials or selected materials to be put online

or on CD as multimedia or other. Then you would get a signed release from the interviewee authorizing you to put the materials or excerpts online. Also find out in whose name the materials are copyrighted and whether you have print and electronic rights to the material or do the owners-authors-interviewees—or you, the videographer-producer? Get it all in writing, signed by those who have given you any interviews, even if you have to call your local intellectual property rights attorney.

#

Chapter Fourteen:

How Accurate Are Autobiographies, Biographies, Personal Histories, Plays and Monologues Based on Life Stories?

Autobiographies, biographies, personal histories, plays, and monologues present a point of view. Are all sides given equal emphasis? Will the audience choose favorite characters? Cameras give fragments, points of view, and bits and pieces. Viewers will see what the videographer or photographer intends to be seen. The interviewee will also be trying to put his point of view across and tell the story from his perspective.

Will the photographer or videographer be in agreement with the interviewee? Or if you are recording for print transcript, will your point of view agree with the interviewee's perspective and experience if your basic 'premise,' where you two are coming from, are not in agreement? Think this over as you write your list of questions. Do both of you agree on your central issue on which you'll focus for the interview?

How are you going to turn spoken words into text for your paper hard copy transcript? Will you transcribe verbatim, correct the grammar, or quote as you hear the spoken words? Oral historians really need to transcribe the exact spoken word. You can leave out the 'ahs' and 'oms' or loud pauses, as the interviewee thinks what to say next. You don't want to sound like a court reporter, but you do want to have an accurate record transcribed of what was spoken.

You're also not editing for a movie, unless you have permission to turn the oral history into a TV broadcast, where a lot gets cut out of the interview for time constraints. For that, you'd need written permission so words won't be taken out of context and strung together in the editing room to say something different from what the interviewee intended to say.

Someone talking could put in wrong names, forget what they wanted to say, or repeat themselves. They could mumble, ramble, or do almost anything. So you would have to sit down and weed out redundancy when you can or decide on presenting exactly what you've heard as transcript.

When someone reads the transcript in text, they won't have what you had in front of you, and they didn't see and hear the live presentation or the videotape. It's possible to misinterpret gestures or how something is spoken, the mood or tone, when reading a text transcript. Examine all your sources. Use an ice-breaker to get someone talking.

If a woman is talking about female-interest issues, she may feel more comfortable talking to another woman. Find out whether the interviewee is more comfortable speaking to someone of his or her own age. Some older persons feel they can relate better to someone close to their own age than someone in high school, but it varies. Sometimes older people can speak more freely to a teenager.

The interviewee must be able to feel comfortable with the interviewer and know he or she will not be judged. Sometimes it helps if the interviewer is the same ethnic group or there is someone present of the same group or if new to the language, a translator is present.

Read some books on oral history field techniques. Read the National Genealogical Society Quarterly (NGSQ). Also look at The American Genealogist (TAG), The Genealogist, and The New England Historical and Genealogical Register (The Register). If you don't know the maiden name of say, your grandmother's mother, and no relative knows either because it wasn't on her death certificate, try to reconstruct the lives of the males who had ever met the woman whose maiden name is unknown.

Maybe she did business with someone before marriage or went to school or court. Someone may have recorded the person's maiden name before her marriage. Try medical records if any were kept. There was no way to find my mother's grandmother's maiden name until I started searching to see whether she had any brothers in this country. She had to have come as a passenger on a ship around 1880 as she bought a farm. Did her husband come with her?

Was the farm in his name? How many brothers did she have in this country with her maiden surname?

If the brothers were not in this country, what countries did they come from and what cities did they live in before they bought the farm in Albany?

If I could find out what my great grandmother's maiden name was through any brothers living at the time, I could contact their descendants perhaps and see whether any male or female lines are still in this country or where else on the globe.

Perhaps a list of midwives in the village at the time is recorded in a church or training school for midwives. Fix the person in time and place. Find out whom she might have done business with and whether any records of that business exist.

What businesses did she patronize? Look for divorce or court records, change of name records, and other legal documents.

Look at local sources. Did anyone save records from bills of sale for weddings, purchases of homes, furniture, debutante parties, infant supplies, or even medical records?

Look at nurses' licenses, midwives' registers, employment contracts, and teachers' contracts, alumni associations for various schools, passports, passenger lists, alien registration cards, naturalization records, immigrant aid societies, city directories, and cross-references.

You might research records at religious and women's clubs, lineage and village societies, girl scouts and similar groups, orphanages, sanatoriums, hospitals, police records. Years ago there was even a Eugenics Record Office. What about the women's prisons? The first one opened in 1839—Mount Pleasant Female Prison, NY.

You may wish to check out voters' lists. If your relative is from another country, try records in those villages or cities abroad. Who kept the person's diaries?

Have you checked the Orphan Train records? Try ethnic and religious societies and genealogy associations for that country. Most ethnic genealogy societies have a special interest group for even the smallest villages in various countries.

You can start one and put up a Web site for people who also come from there in past centuries. Check alimony, divorce, and court records, widow's pensions of veterans, adoptions, orphanages, foster homes, medical records, birth, marriage, and death certificates, social security, immigration, pet license owners' files, prisons, alumni groups from schools, passenger lists, military, and other legal records.

 When all historical records are being tied together, you can add the DNA testing to link all those cousins.

Check military pensions on microfilms in the National Archives. See the bibliography section of this book for further resources on highly recommended books and articles on oral history field techniques and similar historical subjects.

#

Chapter Fifteen:

Reminiscing Your Memoirs or Life Story Highlights with Animation: Write Life Story Experiences as Animated Cartoon Scripts or Use Avatars to Represent Characters in Your Personal History Script

Techniques of writing scripts for cartoon animation also work well when writing life story or personal history scripts. The practice writing springboards, premises, and several drafts polishes your ability to present the highlights of a life story with cartoon animated characters in your computer or online, on disk, or on video. All you have to do is substitute the real person or real personality for the cartoon character, avatar, or robot online, on video, and on disk.

Currently, many animated cartoons are designed overseas, but someone somewhere still has to write the scripts. Here's how to begin. You can write your life story or personal history as an animated cartoon, design animated computer games, including writing the scripts, or think creatively "outside the box." Back in the nineties, writing a life story sometimes featured 'avatars' or computer-generated persona 'robots' online.

Hypertext fiction and life stories flummoxed many in the mid-nineties, but opened new channels of creative expression online. What other media can you use for your life story time capsules? Feature the highlights of significant events in your own life or rites of passage. Keepsakes include your personal journal, video clips and photos, along with DNA-driven genealogy- for-ancestry reports.

How to Write Life Stories as "Saturday-Morning-Type" Cartoons & How to Write

Cartoon Animation Scripts for Multimedia Markets

"You're nearly an octogenarian and counting, but you watch cartoons all morning six days a week?" The audience waited to hear my answer to that person's question. The last time I sniffed salty mouths yawning that wide, they swayed on node hooks at Fisherman's wharf.

That's how people react to the notion that I spent my silver sentinel years writing scripts for animation...life story animation...personal history themes. What does age have to do with it? Nothing, unless you're writing animation scripts for four-year olds or for grown-ups, or writing personal history and life stories as an animation script or illustrated novel.

Writing animation is tougher than writing live-action or dialogue in first person diary novels. You want to put stretch marks on your wallet? Then call every shot in an animation script. You have up to two lines of dialogue before you have to change the shot, the frame, that is. Shot changed already? Then start describing the scene all over again along with what action is happening.

There's no director in animation that will put in the camera angles on your script or other directions. No one will stage your action other than you. Here's your chance to play master of your universe and do everything as the writer in 37-59 pages for a half-hour script that actually runs only 22 minutes.

An animation script takes twice as much writing as a live action screen play. You write two pages of animation for each screen minute. Saturday morning cartoons are the ultimate in teaching tools when transferred to personal history or life stories and to other educational and training materials.

Many writers in animation entered the field decades ago by first writing half-hour television commercials for toys and related educational devices.

Record Cartoons for Study and Analysis

Instead of merely watching cartoons on your TV, record them to tape or DVD. If you're working with tape, stop your video editing device, and freeze a frame. Now write down all the action occurring in that freeze-frame. It should have a beginning, middle, and end-- same as in a short story.

Insert one line of dialogue. Practice writing dialogue from words remembered spoken that you overheard until you become familiar with finding the beginning, middle, and end--the "short story" theme in each freeze-frame. Do you understand what you're looking for--the story line, the action in each frame of animation?

Watch tapes as often as three times a day until the action in each frame becomes familiar as a story with a beginning, middle, and end. There is gold in animation festivals, whether you're writing animation to entertain or writing personal histories in animation format as a way to use your creative expression or as the cliché goes "think outside the box."

Cartoon writers of the eighties and nineties lived in a hyper cubed universe where thinking was done in three dimensions. Today it's action, effects, and visual writing. Only it goes beyond thinking in three dimensions. You have to think inside out. Write in sound effects and write visually. Animation writing is an exercise in highly technical visual thinking. You form a team with the skilled computer artist-animator-designer and the computer engineer.

Learn from TV Toy Ads

Saturday morning cartoons are there to sell toys to children (and parents) who must be persuaded either by their children or by the cartoon ad itself. Watch for the commercials. Sponsors pay for them. Writers can work at the educational materials end of the animation market, write ad copy and dialogue with action for the sponsors, or write the animation for entertainment.

There's another inroad--writing personal life stories and histories, even corporate histories, as animation scripts and illustrated novels. On video or DVD, the animation action and script work together to showcase the highlights of a person's life at any age....or a company's success stories. It all can be a cartoon either for the story itself or to sell as an advertisement, educational materials or a product.

Foreign Animation

In the eighties, when animation began to be sent overseas to be designed, script writers often turned to computer game design and computer game script writing as one alternative. Today many universities have impacted graphic design majors in schools of new media. Computer animation in a variety of countries is shown on TV everywhere. Have you seen the last computer animation from Japan, for example?

What about the 'anime' field and independent producers of animation stories? You could offer animation online and on disk portraying children's life stories for birthday gifts and rites of passage ceremonies. There are so many applications to writing life stories as animation scripts. Only you need a computer animator to be on your team, someone to design the animation art and do the computer editing.

To study animation script writing, hunt for the old cartoon scripts of the thirties and forties. They're rare vintages. Keep a tape or DVD library of dozens of old-time radio programs. Join old-time radio and video clubs online where you can exchange or rent these old cartoons on DVDs or CDs.

Listen to old-time radio shows such as Captain Midnight and The Shadow. Can you write a radio play of someone's life story or personal history in that format--old time radio with special sound effects? If so, put it on a DVD, in your computer and on an external drive. Your goal is to upload your video or audio file to a streaming or downloadable online site. That's one way to create a time capsule, keepsake album, or personal and corporate history that people can access from faraway locations and save as a file in their own devices or computers to play now and in the future as technology evolves.

Watch cartoon animation from other lands. Look at the World War II cartoons shown in local theaters in the forties. They are now on DVDs, online at various video sites, and on VHS tapes that may have been digitized for the changing technology to view on your own video watching devices.

When the recordings deteriorate with time, they are transferred to higher quality media, and whatever comes next after drives, DVDs, and streaming from online sources. You may wish to view the WW 2 themes in the cartoon animation, such as Donald Duck fighting Nazis, which may be uploaded on some sites. Check out the Way Back Machine at Internet Archives, the videos on sites for public viewing, and other sites and media that have saved these historical animation cartoons for public viewing now and hopefully in the future.

For a personal historian, looking at cartoons from other countries at different times can help you learn how propaganda cartoons were used because people thought them to be patriotic. At different periods in history, foreign governments paid for propaganda cartoons that often turn up in archives and libraries. Look at your own country's cartoons from years ago. Was the theme patriotic? In what ways? What did the themes emphasize here, teamwork, for example.

You can make a hobby or research project out of studying the world of animation script writing during various wars, in time, or in geographic space around the world. The themes go beyond the design of animation or the script writing. There are patterns and values in some of these cartoons.

What stories do they tell? What values and virtues? Do they have a purpose, mission, crusade, slogan, proverb, or other message? How do the cartoons impact people, and how do people impact cartoon animation and script writing?

How to Enter the Field of Cartoon Animation Script Writing or Animation of Life Stories and Personal Histories

You may wish to start by either researching the needs of animation design companies or advertising agencies that sponsor the Saturday morning cartoons. Many writers were spiraled into animation script writing from spin-offs of advertising agency electronic ad copywriting and/or graphic illustration jobs.

Some entered animation script writing as former comic-book artists or writers. Others were live-action scriptwriters. Some also are computer game designers. You have the animation artist-designer who turns to script writing. And you have the computer engineer interested in game design. Often cartoon animation design may be outsourced overseas, but what about scriptwriting the dialogue and describing the action and camera angles in animation? Who's doing the voice-overs for the animation characters? Animation on TV for decades has helped to sell toys when the commercials appeared. And various foods for child viewers, such as cereals...

The animation script writer needs the soul of an illustrator even if you don't do visual art work. You can paint pictures with visual writing. The pictures would emphasize action and dialogue. The best way to train is to study paintings in art galleries and museums and watch cartoon animation for exercising the visual side.

On the writing side, you look at cartoon animation scripts and analyze them for story, length, action, dialogue, and appeal to the audience and age level. You also find out whether the script will sell toys or other educational materials and products advertised between the cartoons.

Toy Marketing

Life stories and corporate histories can be marketed as toys, board games, or computer games. Know what age level you'll be targeting. You can even write story books using the lives of your clients who could be children if the parents give information and specify what kind of life story book or cartoon they want with the 'avatar' or "robot image" or photograph of their child.

You work out with the parent what kind of educational life story approach you want to take with animation and script with the family. It makes a fascinating birthday party presentation and gift. From lives to grand openings of stores, you are marketing a toy or a life story with animation script and design.

Here's a very brief history of animation. Between 1984 and 1986 a flood of animation began being turned out for syndication. Through the advertising agency route, animation writers trained on the job to sell toys and women's products. They wrote copy for advertisements and animation scripts. Animation writers marketed toys to children and skin care products primarily to women. The animated script had to sell shampoo, detergents, and bake mixes.

Artists became writers, and writers trained in animation design. Add that group of creative people to a farrago of Hollywood script writers seeking more work or alternatives. Many script writers with degrees in screenwriting turned to the Saturday morning cartoons to make a living. College campuses began to offer courses in animation and later, new media animation such as desktop video animation and new media writing.

The Boom and the Bust

A tremendous amount of animation flooded the markets around 1986. By 1987, the boom turned to bust, leaving many writers by 1988 vying for what assignments and contracts came their way by the time the Internet brought new hope to the nineties and beyond. The good news is that those who had been writing animation scripts leaped into writing live-action screen plays or went into multimedia educational design and writing. Others went into Web design and online digital journalism. Still others sought out print-on-demand publishing venues.

Breaking into cartoon animation can take one to five years. Collaboration is common. Often you find work through the multimedia and other computer-related markets. I found work as an independent contractor writing success stories and case histories for a software manufacturer at the end of the nineties. There is a bright side.

Animation Writing Agents

Since writing animation pays no residuals, newcomers are given a second chance if they get the go-ahead to write a sample script. Prime-time TV won't touch you without an agent. So without an agent, you need to pitch a few seconds in writing to a story editor at your chosen animation studio.

You first phone the various studios and independent producers and ask for the name of the story editor. Then you talk to the story editor or pitch in writing. It's the story editor who has the power to work with you and is your first link to the industry. First you have to pitch a story, and most often the story line is related to the cartoon show's 'bible.' The 'bible' is a reference and resource book of what the characters are like and what they do in a particular cartoon show on TV.

If you live out of town from where the studio is located, tell the story editor that you have a computer and can send the script electronically. It can go by email. Most studios have bulletin boards to which you can download or upload all types of pitches, springboards, treatments, stories, and scripts.

Telecommuting

The computer bulletin board for animation writers in the 1980s was called "*The Algonquin Board.*" Its private number and mailing address appealed to members because the only way to become a member was to have someone in the industry recommend you.

You were in a position that sometimes the only way in was to accept an assignment on speculation and then ask your story editor to recommend you as a member. Otherwise, you were left to introduce yourself at professional meetings by volunteering for such types of organizations.

Today, you can check out the many associations and unions for animation writers that are listed online. Network with the many associations listed as links at: *The Electronic Media and Film* (as a major) Web site of Towson University, Electronic Media & Film Department, Towson,

MD. Or see the Web site:
http://www.towson.edu/emf/links.htm. The website at this time reads, *"The Electronic Media and Film Department engages a new generation of enthusiastic artists, entertainers and communicators to share media in bold and unconventional new ways."*

What you want to look for on bulletin and message boards or email lists of related associations are job information, marketing ideas, and professional resources. Join associations and volunteer to interview people. Write articles for the association's newsletter or other publications.

Mailing lists and bulletin boards online may have job information and valuable resources. Meet people and find out whether they want to spread the news about what they are doing in the field. Write success stories.

Meet other writers and story editors at trade and professional associations in the field of writing for animation. Back in the eighties, there was a bulletin board that served live-action screenwriters called the Wicked Scherzo Board, but back then, the only way to get phone numbers of members was to ask a member in the industry to recommend you.

You need not have sold a script at that time. Today, most networking is done in various universities departments of electronic media and film with industry internships and professional associations as members volunteer to work on newsletters and at conventions and conferences to 'network.'

Instead of meeting only writers, try to network with musicians, artists, engineers, special effects designers, and technicians who work in the computer animation industry. It's all about teamwork, and every artist needs a script to animate. Check out the advertising agencies, educational publishers and producers, trainers, corporate industrial film producers, and comic book publishers for their writing needs.

Then there are the radio scripts for Internet broadcast or multicast. Elementary school teachers can use plays for puppet shows as well as the producers of the puppet shows for schools. Everyone works with some kind of script presenting to students or at weddings and other celebrations, and scripts have themes or niche markets. Also try the ethnic and religious markets.

Working with Nets: One way to meet people in the animation and script writing industries is to join the International Animated Film Association

(ASIFA). The Web site for Hollywood at this date is at: http://www.asifa-hollywood.org/. The International Web site for ASIFA is at: http://www.asifa.net/.

There are national and international chapters

The Los Angeles headquarters of ASIFA may be able to help you reach people employed at the various studios in the vicinity of Hollywood. Call the studios directly and speak to the story editors. Check the Encyclopedia of Associations in your public library for a long list of animation associations worldwide or look on the Web at www.google.com or other search engines for more associations. Some offer workshops with networking. Stay in communication with the various studios in Los Angeles.

Contact the story editors each month, and ask them to send you animation scripts. You can write to them and enclose self-addressed stamped envelopes. Never pester them or call too frequently. Bring to the story editors your related stories and your unique scripts. To prepare, read the animation scripts. Analyze the scripts. Study the scripts to see what was emphasized and find out why those scripts were accepted and satisfactory. Those topics give you factual material to discuss with the story editors.

As story editors to send you the 'bibles' of various animation characters you select. This 'bible' is a book several inches thick that tells everything you need to know about the cartoon character. If you write life stories as cartoon animation, then you'll need to make such a 'scrap book' or 'bible' on the person about whose life you are writing.

Learn all you can about the cartoon character and his henchmen from the cartoon bible. Make yourself valuable to studio officials. Ask them what already has been pitched. Ask what titles have sold the quickest. Ask kids what makes them laugh. Ask older adults what makes them laugh. Ask kids what they want to see on television cartoons. Ask people of all ages what they would like to see of their own life stories on TV cartoons, even if the TV set is from their own DVD disk of their life story or other significant event.

Ask the story editor what are the taboos. The bible and sample scripts will let you know in general, but if you miss a point, ask. There are several types of cartoon shows on TV, the hard and the soft.

Hard and Soft TV Animation Shows

There are soft and hard cartoon animation shows on TV. Soft shows don't have too much action adventure. Write sample scripts of each type. The hard shows have the "hit 'em hard" characters that enjoy things that people can't do legally.

Do you really enjoy your characters torching toy stores as in the cartoon, Robocop? Or would you prefer to go inward into your imagination and write a zoo story? Look at scripts from the soft animation shows produced during the eighties such as Jim Henson's Muppet Babies.

You might want to watch the old cartoons and compare the action on screen with the written script. The scripts often are available from the story editors, animation writers' associations, and also from stores in Hollywood that sell old scripts. In the eighties when I was writing sample animation scripts, the story editors from the various studios sent me their 'bible' and sample scripts for various shows.

Chances are no one will buy your sample scripts. You might want to focus writing life story scripts to be later put into computer animation with a variety of animation software. Sample scripts for particular shows that no one buys are not a total waste. They are used as part of your resume.

You show a story editor your sample script along with your resume. These samples show the story editors that you know the format. You learn to format a story, and you learn to structure a story. It's one way to showcase your 'handle' on credible cartoon dialogue.

Pitching

Introduce yourself by phone to the story editor. Find out whether they also take email queries. It's more personal by phone if not in person. Tell the story editor that you have a sample script to send. Give your verbal pitch in 20 seconds.

Then tell the story editor that you'll send the required written pitch. Find out whether they want the pitch emailed or sent by regular mail.

The story editor will probably say your idea has been pitched. However, if your story line has a fresh angle, you'll me asked to mail it in. Here's your chance to be creative and still stick to the 'bible' or script requirements for a particular show.

Springboard

You first send the story editor a half-page, double-spaced bare-bones summary called a springboard. Every story can be pared to a half-page bare bones summary. Look at it as if it were the marketing material that goes on the back cover of your story.

Think of the springboard as the back-cover marketing description of your novel designed to hook the reader. It is there to make the story editor want to open your book or actually read more of your script. You will not be paid to write a springboard.

After you have written this half-page double-spaced springboard containing the bare bones of your script or story, you will be asked to write a premise. So, if the editor likes your springboard and assigns you a premise to write, you will be paid for the premise.

Premise

A premise is a two-page, double-spaced, expanded springboard. Make your premise a story with a beginning, middle, and end. Every frame and sequence of your story needs a beginning, middle, and end. Your premise needs to contain the hook that the story editor will use to sell your idea to the networks or to clients.

Cartoons have paid advertising sponsors. They are aired to sell the sponsor's toys. The most important point that can sell your episode for a Saturday morning cartoon is its title.

Work on your title to make it salable. If you're writing a life story as an animation script for use on DVDs, flash drives, external drives, online sites, or computers, keep the title pertinent and short. Often familiar titles sell well, especially in first editions.

Give your play, skit, animation script, or dramatization of a life story event a title that makes an impact. Example: Murphy's Law is familiar. Choose something similarly familiar to most people for your title.

Titles that resemble popular, ageless songs also sell. Talk to your story editor about what is expected or taboo in the title. Look at the best hundred titles that have sold cartoons. What does the story editor or clients like about those titles?

Outline

Once the network or client approves your premise, you will be paid to write an outline. Be specific. Break the action down frame by frame and scene by scene. Use hardly any dialogue at all. Your outline runs between eight and 12 pages in length if you are writing for a half-hour show--which is actually only 22 minutes of screen time.

First Draft

When the story editor approves your outline, you move to the first draft of your script. There's always the first draft followed by the revisions. There may be one or two writers assigned to the script. One writer may be credited with the story and one or two more with the script.

Bumped Off

Before you agree to write any material for pay, you'll be handed a "work for hire" agreement to sign. At any stage, you may be "bumped off." That means being cut off with no more pay or credits. Once you are cut off by the studio it can give your premise or outline to any other writer or shelve your work permanently. You could be paid for your premise and then cut off. Or this could happen as you hand in your outline, in which case you'll be paid for the outline.

How Much?

Payments vary with each studio. Some pay 40 percent of the script fee if you're cut off at outline. The minimum fee for a half-hour script at several studies started at slightly more than

$3,000. For network shows, payment could range from $4,000 to $6,000 or more, depending upon your experience.

What Are You Worth?

Make yourself valuable to studio officials. Ask them what has been pitched in the past. Ask what titles sold the quickest. Talk to children. Ask kids what makes them laugh.

When and if asked, you may wish to send studios a collection or database of children's reactions to cartoons when you are asking for work. A child's creativity has not been discouraged by rejection. Children don't have writer's block. Comic strip writers, filmmakers, teachers, and anthropologists also can be resources.

Research Comic Books

Many former writers of comic book stories and similar novels have become animation script writers. Talk to the people who write and draw the comic books and their publishers and editors. Many cartoon shows are based on comic-book or comic-strip heroes and heroines.

Some scripts are spin-offs of live-action TV programs. The eighties saw Robocop and Star Trek take off in a variety of media from novels to cartoons. Animation writing is a collaborative effort. Firms that publish comic books also may have animation studios on the opposite coast.

Animation Scripts Use Comic-Book Style Dialogue and Descriptive Language

The same descriptive language used in comic strips is written into animation scripts. For example, you'll see the heavy use of sound effects (SFX) in most lines of description and dialogue in adventure-action cartoons. Animation scripting is mostly description of action and hardly any dialogue at all.

Comic Conventions

Attend the comic conventions in your sit, and sit on the "writing for animation" panel. Create your own panel at conferences and conventions for people in similar industries. Phone and write to experts you will be researching or interviewing for articles you may write in a newsletter of one of the trade or professional associations.

Ask the experts to come and join you on a panel at a convention or conference or a class or group meeting. An example would be a writer's club or a film society. The topic could be on how to write for the animation industry.

Comic Books: Writing Life Stories as Graphic Novels or in 32-page Comic Book Formats

Life stories can be presented as comic books. That's one alternative. Another is writing for the animation industry or speaking about that industry by researching comic books. Talk to people who work at home with computer and Internet connection writing cartoon scripts. Ask these experts to be on your panel at conferences such as comic book publishers' conventions or seminars on writing for the new media. A comic book format doesn't have to contain material designed to make readers laugh. It can hold real life stories using graphics and dialogue with a little description in cartoon format.

Timing Is Important

Most cartoon shows are picked up by studios in February. Call various studios during the month when they are pitching network shows. Exceptions to the February pickup rule included the old 1980s shows such as *The Smurfs* (Hanna-Barbera) and *Fraggle Rock* or the *Muppet Babies* (Marvel) which had early pick-ups. *Alf* was produced at Disney Studios in Burbank, California. There were a wide variety of shows decades ago such as *Pee Wee's Playhouse*. What about today? More life stories in caricature, like *South Park* and the *Simpsons* of the new millennium.

The persons in charge of development (as well as the producers) are listed in the credits that roll at the end of each cartoon show. Record the cartoons for your personal research and find out who is the appropriate person to query regarding writing springboards or other materials. Sometimes a producer needs public relations material written. That's another side door into the industry, through public relations work on the cartoon shows or with the sponsors. Multimedia animation studies are another door that may offer internships.

The mid-eighties was one of the "golden ages" of Saturday morning cartoon shows on TV when freelance script writers had the chance to walk in and present their writing to story editors or to telephone from anywhere. You didn't necessarily have had to live in Los Angeles to be a cartoon script writer. Today with Internet multimedia, you can produce life stories or corporate histories yourself and present them as animated cartoon shows or other types of multimedia presentations such as time capsules.

What you need to search for is the 'downtime' at the studios of your choice. That downtime is a good time to talk to story editors about writing sample scripts, obtaining 'bibles' and other materials you'll need to begin your springboard for a particular show. Your one best sample script can be used to sell many shows at several studios.

#

Chapter Sixteen:

Turning Life Story Vignettes, Plays and Skits into Computer and Board Games

The goal of fiction writers in the new media is to adapt your story, novel, or script to as many platforms, formats and media as possible and to sell to multiple markets--either online, multi-casting, or multimedia. Computer game scripts aren't only for computer games anymore.

They're used in dramatizations for training and learning simulations and other learning materials as well as for entertainment online, on disk, and for infotainment and edutainment at all levels from corporate training to Web sites for children and young adults, seniors, and students.

Here's how to write a computer game script that you can adapt to any type of simulation training or interactive learning as well as entertainment fiction. The average computer screen interactive video or game has double the number of camera directions as a regular video script. The increased number of descriptions account for the camera directions and the director's directions (since you're the director and the writer on the computer as you are in animation).

So to adapt your screenplay to the new media, separate the beginning, middle and ending exactly as you would cut off the beginning, middle, and ending of a short story or novel. In a screenplay, every scene forms a creative concept. In the industry, the executives try to separate the one-line high concept from the whole-story-based creative concept.

A creative concept is a basic device that's used like an all-encompassing net to catch all the important events of the story. Think of your creative concept as a Native American dream catcher net full of feathers and beads woven into memories and facts of your story. A dream catcher style to a creative concept can grab the audience's attention and squeeze until it gives pleasure or emotional response, like fear. But you may want to send a specific message in your reminisce therapy writing that focuses on life story experiences.

Summarize the highlights into a single paragraph that tells the story. In a screenplay, it has been said and for the past two decades been written about that you divide your story into three acts. However, in adapting a script or story to the new interactive media, you don't divide it into three acts, and you don't divide it into six acts. You bring out eight octopus-sized tentacles or branches and you hang your computer game script or interactive book story on those eight branches.

It has been said that at each new path, or what the screenplay books of the seventies used to call turning points, a new crisis happens that propels the action in forward. However, in the new media, each new crisis instead propels the action down another branching pathway, through another road, and into another narrative.

Again, the reader chooses when the action is supposed to branch and turn on its dime to move forward in not so much a new direction, but in the direction the reader says it will move. The writer no longer chooses. Interactively, the reader chooses.

If you need to write a premise and introduce your hero, in an interactive script you adapt your old media book by writing a summary of the end first and then working backwards to the first chapter or the first page. Interactive books are adapted by writing back starting with the end of the book, story, or script and shuffling the deck.

The crisis that sets the story in motion is never limited to only one crisis, but eight, or four, or two, or some other even number. Let the reader choose the crisis the viewer wants to work with, and give more than one summary of each chapter. You adapt a life story to a play, skit, monologue, or script to the new media by working backwards from the end of the adventure.

Here are some problems to solve as you write your dramatizations for training scripts online or computer game scripts:

•   In a nonfiction interactive script, find your biggest weapon to slay the problem that has to be solved in the action of your nonfiction script. This cliffhanger approach is good when you're writing a how-to training video, film, or CD-ROM learning tool.

- Create a high-stakes races to hook your cliffhanger on.

- Find a new acronym for each 7-minute scene in your script and lay your cliffhanger on at the end of each 7-8 minute segment of a nonfiction script.

- If you're looking for a cover-all that makes your script hang together, use the cliffhanger to make a connection between what's a household name in your script, the problem to be solved, and the method your narrator or main character uses in the dramatization to solve the problem and reach a conclusion.

- Sell your cliffhangers to the interactive TV market targeting ADSL (asymmetric digital subscriber line) technology. ADSL is high bandwidth Internet connectivity that you can use to bring your script to commercial quality video on the Web. Use videoconferencing as a means to transmit your scripts to a live audience interested in nonfiction - that is problem solving, skill training, test taking/preparation, and feedback at business meetings.

- Use wireless paths to sell your cliffhangers, and use cliffhangers in training videos and videoconferencing. The phone companies are eager to get into the interactive TV business.

•	Write scripts about bandwidth itself for a technical audience as practice, using cliffhangers every 7-8 minutes as paths provided for the narrator to take new action and move the script faster until a problem is solved at the end and the skill is learned by the corporate employee or student watching your script.

•	Have your script read before a live audience or through videoconferencing and have the audience decide which cliffhangers to insert at each point. Use about 8 cliffhangers per instructional film script.

•	Cliffhangers can be used in nonfiction comic books or graphic instructional materials. Most comic books are 32 pages in length. Double that size to 64 pages and you come out with a script for a computer game lasting 22 minutes or more. You also get a graphic novel at that length or a booklet on how to perform a special skill.

The competing cliffhangers grow in volume as the story moves forward, even if it's a routine safety instructional film to train vehicle drivers.

Test your cliffhangers' performance. Set up a Web site and get feedback from your cliffhangers from an audience. Try before you make your cliffhangers permanent.

 You're teaching even if you're not writing anything instructional in the traditional sense. Propaganda films teach a lesson, too. You get at the emotional response of the audience through cliffhangers.

Then you appeal to their thinking, logical side to insert the facts that come after the cliffhanger. The narrator, the product, or the audience can become involved n the cliffhanger and solve the problem to get the answer. Use mazes when appropriate.

Even mazes can become cliffhangers, and text mazes of logic are useful only when you are teaching the viewer to use test methods to solve problems. Write cliffhangers as plays. Use more emotion than you would in a film script. Don't insist the audience will think if they are looking to escape and feel. You're not writing a film script with outdoor action. Most people view a script to have fun and learn by passive imprinting and associations rather than to be forced to solve problems.

Therefore, let the dramatized character solve the cliffhanger/problem. A cliffhanger is a substitute for a problem to be solved in a nonfiction script. In a fiction script, a cliffhanger is hidden problem to be solved and exposed suspense requiring emotional reactions to solve.

Ten Steps to Dramatizing Interactive Personal Essays as Plays

1.   Ask a specific question.

2.   Use the essay to answer the question.

3.   Write the question at the start of the essay and make your question interactive inserting many branches or possibilities each possibility narrowing down more and more to concentrate your reader's mind.

4.   Use the interactivity to ask the reader how does this paragraph help answer the question?

5.   Whenever the paragraph finishes answering the question begin a new branching narrative, pathway, or choice for the reader. It's time for a break of concentration and a shifting to a cliff-hanger.

6.   Even the brief personal essays in interactive media can have cliffhangers, even in

nonfiction, autobiography, and other personal essays based on life experience. Many experiences can lead to a topic for writing in any media, such as how to receive email interviews.

7.	Another fiction with a real-life practical use online topic you can make a script or article from is how to get terrific email interviews. Books can be written from lists such as a list fleshed out of what are the funniest things that happened to employers recruiting employees on the Internet, such as viruses that came with resumes. Base your writing on interviews with dozens of human resources personnel who hire people from the Internet based on resumes and correspondence coming in my email and from Web page recruiting.

8.	A writer gets all interviews for a book from the Internet. I once wrote a book based on interviews all gotten by email. I requested the interview by email and got the person on the other side to give me the interview by email only.

9.	Most of my interviews in the past were with famous and best selling authors and screenwriters, including interviews with big-name screenwriters who switched to writing for the new media (like Ken Goldstein, publisher/screenwriter of the Carmen San Diego series for Broderbund), and best selling interactive novel writers/publishers, and virtual press publishers.

10.   You could write a computer game, animation script, essay or an article or book on how to get great interviews by email for any writer who is working on a book or a column. Your title could be: Secrets of Success in Email Interviewing. What\'s the funniest thing that happened to you on the Internet while writing your column or other creative writing?

#

Interview from the 1990s:

Jeffrey Sullivan of DigitalArcana, Inc.

http://www.DigitalArcana.com

Q. What outlook do you see in interactive multimedia for freelance fiction and/or nonfiction writers as far as making a living, opening a writing service or home-based business, or getting a job?

A. There is tremendous opportunity for writers (both fiction and non-fiction) in the area of interactive media. The incredible growth in the market has spawned a strong appetite for new talent, and the increasing market shares in the more mature sub-markets mean some increase in pay rates. Building a career in this field remains a fantastic opportunity, but there are some things to remember:

1.   Know your field. Don't just hop on the bandwagon because you hear interactive is "the next hot thing." Not only will it be easy for potential employers to sniff this out, but it's the absolute worst thing you can do, both for your personal employment opportunities, and for opportunities for writers in general.

2.   One of the biggest problems In interactive is that there are a lot of "displaced writers" from other media who figure that "writing is writing," so they just hop into interactive, over-promise what they can do in this tricky medium, and leave producers with a bad taste in their mouth for "professional writers."

3.   The newer the field, the more appetite, but the less the pay (in general). If you want to be on the cutting edge, be prepared to pay the dues.

4.   Love this stuff. If you're just in it for a paycheck, then #1-2 above will ensure that you not only flop, but that you make it harder for other writers to follow you.

Solid writing skills is something I'll take as a given (if you don't have it, I can't tell you how to get it). Experience is easy to acquire. Go out there and use the products you want to create. If it's adventure games, play adventure games ravenously. If it's edutainment, then experience all of them out there.

One caveat: don't just check out the "hot" titles in a field. There's nothing worse than hearing a person rattle off the two or three best known entries in a field as their favorites, a sure sign that they haven't done their homework. (A side note: if I had a dime for every time I heard someone tell me they had an idea for a cross between "Doom" and "MYST" over the past few years, I'd be independently wealthy.)

Q. For the older writer - 55+ - who has been rejected by ageism from the Hollywood screenwriting market, or for the novelist seeking a publisher, what does interactive multimedia offer?

A. I hate to say this, but in many of the interactive fields, ageism is even worse in interactive. In all of the "hot" areas like cutting-edge gaming and interactive fiction, there is a fairly strong perception that anyone over the age of 30 (!) doesn't "get it," and can't write this stuff.

The perception is that well-established linear writers simply can't think non-linearly as interactive often requires. However, I think that in the fields of reference, education, and entertainment, there may be much less of this attitude. Since my experience lies elsewhere, however, I can't be sure.

How would a freelance writer of fiction or nonfiction who has been doing print writing for years begin to make the leap to get into writing interactive multimedia? Are there any jobs out there for writers who can't find work on daily newspapers because of the downsizing of daily newspapers?

If you're a newspaper writer, your best entree into interactive may be with the marketing department of an interactive company; there your skills are the most directly relevant. Once you're in, you can absorb the culture and experience, and try to branch out into other areas.

For general writers, the key is knowing the field. Know as much as you can about what has worked (and what has not) in your field, and know why things work or don't, in your opinion. Knowledgeable people in this field are rare, so preparing yourself is a great way to get that foot a little farther in the door.

Q. What advice would you give to creative writers of all types to enter the new media?

A. Know the area you want to work in exhaustively. And try to know the other areas at least in passing. You never know where a good idea (or even a bad one) in one field will yield a great innovation in another.

Q. Is there anything readers might want to know about the hidden markets in interactive multimedia? Can one work at home?

A. Working at home is a definite option in many cases. Interactive firms, being much more highly computerized in general, are a lot more comfortable with the concept of telecommuting or simply working off-site than many other industries.

Q. Is it easier to sell to the interactive multimedia market than to try to find a print publisher for one's novel, screenplay, or how-to nonfiction book?

A. No. With respect to a book, you can create what is essentially the finished product. With respect to a screenplay, even though the script isn't the finished product, the accepted convention is that writers don't do anything more than a script. In interactive, however, the norm is to need to do a prototype or sample art in addition to a design document, so there is more to do to get an idea sold. Add to that the fact that many companies have more ideas than they can handle, and the market for new ideas is not as great as it once was.

Q. What education is best for a freelance creative writer to get a foot in the door in the new media? A background in computers, writing, game playing (if you're interested in the game market)? Can a writer educate himself at home and work at home, or must there be a college degree with a major in interactive multimedia to enter the occupation of writer in this field? In other words, will a B.A. in English get one in the door? What other job titles are there in interactive multimedia for writers? What else can they do in this field to find work? How long have writers been writing for interactive multimedia? Five years? Three years?

A. Absolutely not. For one thing, these college degrees are so new that there are few people in the market who will even have one.

Second, this industry values credits and experience over degrees more than many other fields. The more technical your interest, however, the more likely that a degree will be necessary.

Q. What's the future of multimedia for freelance creative writers?

I think that creative people will be the guiding force in moving interactive media into a new and mature mass-medium. Technology can only take you so far, and although we've been driven by it so far, it is becoming harder and harder to differentiate your product on technology alone.

Soon, it will be impossible. The companies know this, but they are often caught between two cultures (technology driving product and content driving product); soon their minds will be made up for them.

\#

Chapter Seventeen:

Stimulating and Enhancing Memories

Does Writing Your Life Story As A Play for High-School Students or Older Adults Help Refresh Memories?

Keys: 1. Plug in characters to a variety of experiences. 2. Research several ways to tell the same story.

Monologues, plays, and oral histories depend upon memory and the ability to speak. I also think of oral history as aural history, based on the ability to hear someone's experiences and remember them to pass on to the next generation or the world.

To find out the effects of oral history on memory and on creative writing of plays, skits, or stories on memory, we'd have to ask the people who write their life story and/or genealogy in their older years what it did for them, their memory, and their ability to think and feel. Make use of introverted feeling in writing a commercial or salable life story for the new media. Think in three dimensions for older adults is a different highway. How did DNA testing influence a genealogy search for family history facts?

Did the individual create a time capsule? How was the time capsule saved—on the Web? On a disc or drive, on a DVD, video uploaded online, or audio files? In a scrapbook of photos, with various memorabilia? Did anyone rescue old photos from antique stores and flea markets by searching for photographer's prints on the front or back of the photo or names on the back of the photo and dates or locations?

1. When turning your salable life story, corporate history, or biography into an adventure action romance novel, don't set up your main characters in the first chapter to be in transit traveling on board a plane, train, or ship going somewhere. The action actually starts or hits them after they have already arrived at their destination.

Start your first chapter when your characters already arrive at their destination place or point in time. A first chapter that opens when your main character is on a plane or train is the kiss of death from many editors point of view and the main reason why a good novel often is rejected.

Cut out the traveling scene from your first chapter and begin where the action starts for real, at the destination point. Does anyone visit antique stores, malls, or flea markets to search for family history memorabilia? What about attic, basement, or garage sales?

2. Use a lot of dialogue when turning a biography or your life story into a salable novel, especially in a romance, adventure action, or suspense novel or in one where you combine romance with adventure and suspense.

Use no more than three pages of narrative without dialogue. Let characters speak through the dialogue and tell the reader what is happening. Get characters to speak as normally as possible. If the times and place dictate they speak in proverbs, so be it. Proverbs make the best novels as you turn your proverb into a story and play it out as a novel. Otherwise, have normal speech so you can be the catalyst and bring people together who understand clearly what one another means.

3. Put your characters on the stage and have them talking to one another. If you have introspection in your book, don't use introspection for your action line. Action adventure books keep characters on stage talking to the audience.

4. Use magazines and clothing catalogues to make a collage of what your character might look like. This inspiration may go up on a board in front of you or on the wall to see as you work. Get a picture in your mind of what your characters look like. If they don't exist in art history, draw them yourself or make a mixed media collage of what they look like, speak like, and stand for. Some ideas include the models in "cigar" magazines, catalogues, and fashion publications as well as multi-ethnic and historical illustrations and photos.

5. Research history and keep a loose-leaf notebook with tabs on the history of places you want to research. The history itself is great for ideas on what plot to write. Look at or visit old forts and similar places. Plug in characters to your research. Look at forts of foreign settlements in the country of your choice, U.S. or any other place. Record the dates in your files. Create a spreadsheet in Excel or any other type of spread sheet with your dates from historical research as these will relate to your characters and help you develop a real plot.

6. Keep a notebook for each novel or biography you write. Put everything related to each book in a notebook. Have one notebook for historical research and one for the novel you're writing or true storybook.

7. When sending out your book manuscript make a media kit for yourself with your resume, photo, list of works in development if you are not yet published, and any other material about your own experience in any other field. Your own biography and photo presented to the press also can be used to let an editor know when you send out your manuscript of what's in development and what you've done.

8. Write down the point of view before your book is begun. Whose point of view is it anyway? Who tells the story? If you're writing a romance novel from your life story or a military romantic suspense novel, true story, radio script, or other genre, agree on the point of view before you start.

9. Who will tell the story, and how does the individual know how the other characters know what to say?

10. It is not necessary to continue ethnic stereotypes in your book. If one of your characters is a music agent, for example, and a lot of music agents are of one ethnicity or speak with a certain accent, it's not necessary to continue the stereotyping roles. Pick something new for a change.

11. Cliché use evokes familiarity, especially in a title. Research many different ways to tell the same story. Use plays, skits, monologues, dramatizations, diaries, novels, stories, and essays. Viewers and readers need to grasp facts or experiences, anecdotes, oral histories, and stories that have not been generalized. Use a series of incidents, action and relationship tension to balance your plot with your dialogue. Transcribe recorded oral histories. Use a release form that releases you from liability resulting from any public viewing.

12. If you're turning a biography into a romance novel, you need to balance the relationship tension with the mystery, action, or other plot. You must have some event occur on both sides, on the sexual tension side and on the mystery or action side to balance out the book.

Writing Multimedia Plays for High-School Students and Older Adults

What kind of training would a writer need to write real life story plays for multimedia or Internet Broadcasting?

The three key ingredients are solid experience in the following genres:

1.   Writing or adapting plays, skits, and monologues from real life stories.

2.   Working with interactive literature and multimedia skills.

3.   Oral and personal history interviewing skills.

#

Record and Transcribe Life Stories as Highlights, Turning Points, Skits, or Significant Events:

Recording and transcribing personal histories in their original form and/or as skits, plays, monologues, stories, novels, and memoirs are team projects of the person whose life is being turned into a time capsule and for the personal historian with a video camera, tape recorder, and notepad.

For every action in a life story, there's an equal and opposite reaction that's primarily character-driven and secondarily plot-driven. And in an autobiography or anyone's life story, relationship tension occurs. Then the plot moves on. You may not use the entire life history, but only highlights, events, experiences, and excerpts, stages of life and rites of passages.

If it's a romantic suspense or mystery within a life story, such as true confession, true crime, or biography, usually twenty-four short chapters makes a book-length story. Note how the memories are brought up by associations with various words, places, or questions.

A diary is written in first person as a journal or log, but a biography can be of you or your client. Even in a memoirs book or diary, you have to balance action with interaction between the heroine and the hero.

You can be the only person in your diary, but the action and interaction needs to be balanced with something out there in the external world—either forces of nature or another person—or the competition.

If you keep the competition out of your diary, put in the memories, actions, and warmth of the friends, including pets. If there are no other people, put in some force of spirit, some other push and pull, or tension, for balance with something outside yourself. This can be a job, school, a hobby, or what you choose as the force that pulls in an opposite direction existing with the force or person that pulls in your direction.

Try putting the relationship tension between the hero and heroine in the even-numbered chapters, and the mystery, historical events, or action plot events in the odd-numbered chapters.

In a 24-chapter- historical romance, this alternating action chapter, romantic tension chapter balances the plot smoothly. Most historical romance novels have 22-24 chapters.

If you analyze the best-selling ones, you'll see that chapter one has an opening scene on the action side so you see what's happening.

The first action-oriented introductory chapter that shows us what's happening is followed by the second chapter on the romantic tension side showing us when and how the heroine meets the hero or has a re-union with the hero. In the second chapter, the writer takes the heroine somewhere in place or time. The heroine in the second chapter is defined. Either she's a 90's woman, or she's in her place in history or rebelling against it. You tell the story. If you're male, you'd use a hero.

Romantic life stories featuring genealogy combined with biography usually are 10-12 chapters long. Historical romances are twice that size at 22-24 chapters. The writer decides whether it's best to turn a biography into a historical romance or a life story into a mystery, suspense, action adventure, young adult novel, romance, or other genre.

If you are not fictionalizing genealogy or biography into a story, keep your time capsule book, database, or other media true to facts and historical records only. You might want to add your DNA testing records of relatives along with a family tree or other database or time capsule.

For those who want to turn factual biography into a novel, in turning a biography into a romance, the romantic tension side is about girl meeting hero in the first chapter. In the second chapter, the hero takes her somewhere in place, space, time, or state of mind. An oral history may be written as true life story in the form of a novel or play, skit, or anecdote of experience.

The oral history highlights a life experience within a time frame set in one or more locations with all the nuances of that place. It's basically a life story, but it can be transcribed with that certain something, including—charisma, liveliness, action, forward movement, drama, tension, and unique experiences, problems solved, and goals.

#

Chapter Eighteen

Why Reminisce Therapeutically or Write Personal Histories/Life Stories to Stimulate Memory and Build Your Own Dialogue Mirror Using Multimedia?

Joy exists in writing about what holds importance to the author. Memoirs writing is about using words to describe your ability to react, then to act. Through writing from memories, although memories may not always be accurate, is to raise and rebuild your own inner laughing wall.

By writing memoirs you gain insight into yourself so you can find closure or no longer think with the logic of the psychically impaled. Memoirs can help you take out some of the knots in your life.

The act of writing your life story as columns, anecdotes, vignettes, skits, monologues, plays, novels, stories, poetry, or designs may offer insight into your mind and will. It can be a way to prevent you from trapping yourself between any family's love and their ridicule.

By writing your memoirs, you can become the child again who deserves your love. Truth becomes concrete. Intuition evolves into resource.

Yet--if by writing your life story highlights you were to create wombs in men, caverns of deep, physical thinking, then what would you risk? Absolute power over your own mind? The search for identity is only one part of the whole universal shebang.

Memoirs give you strength and nourishment. Growing up means always having to revise. And with blessed retirement, comes the opportunity revise under your own direction within your memoirs. You, at last, remain in your writing, boss of your own creativity. Who needs polarity when you can experience irony by observing? You can seek joy of life through metaphor.

You can seek visual anthropology through journalism. Why be abstract when you can be concrete and write through and with the senses—including the sixth sense of intuition?

You can view life up close or remotely from an armchair. Why view when you can have insight, hindsight, and foresight?

Why observe as a journalist, when you can read how to avoid the pitfalls from ethnographers? Live the design-driven life. And the design-driven life has a purpose: To inspire and motivate persistence through memoir.

#

Appendix A:

Ethnic Genealogy Web Sites

(Usually, there are several genealogy sites on the Web for each ethnic group.)

Acadian/Cajun: & French Canadian:
http://www.acadian.org/tidbits.html

Afghanistan Genealogy:
http://www.kindredtrails.com/afghanistan.html

African-American:
http://www.cyndislist.com/african.htm

African Royalty Genealogy:
http://www.uq.net.au/~zzhsoszy/

Albanian Research List:
http://feefhs.org/al/alrl.html

Armenian Genealogical Society:
http://feefhs.org/am/frg-amgs.html

Asia and the Pacific:
http://www.cyndislist.com/asia.htm

Austria-Hungary Empire:
http://feefhs.org/ah/indexah.html

Baltic-Russian Information Center:
http://feefhs.org/blitz/frgblitz.html

Belarusian—Association of the Belarusian
Nobility: http://feefhs.org/by/frg-zbs.html

Bukovina Genealogy:
http://feefhs.org/bukovina/bukovina.html

Carpatho-Rusyn Knowledge Base:
http://feefhs.org/rusyn/frg-crkb.html

Chinese Genealogy:
http://www.chineseroots.com

Croatia Genealogy Cross Index:
http://feefhs.org/cro/indexcro.html

Czechoslovak Genealogical Society Int'l, Inc.:
http://feefhs.org/czs/cgsi/frg-cgsi.html

Eastern Europe:
http://www.cyndislist.com/easteuro.htm

Eastern European Genealogical Society, Inc.:
http://feefhs.org/ca/frg-eegs.html

Eastern Europe Ethnic, Religious, and National Index with Home Pages includes the FEEFHS Resource Guide that lists organizations associated with FEEFHS from 14 Countries. It also includes Finnish and Armenian genealogy resources: http://feefhs.org/ethnic.html

Ethnic, Religious, and National Index 14 countries: http://feefhs.org/ethnic.html

(Finland) Genealogical Society of Finland:
http://www.genealogia.fi/indexe.htm

Finnish Genealogy Group:
http://feefhs.org/misc/frgfinmn.html

Galicia Jewish SIG: http://feefhs.org/jsig/frg-gsig.html

German Genealogical Digest:
http://feefhs.org/pub/frg-ggdp.html

Greek Genealogy Sources on the Internet:
http://www-personal.umich.edu/~cgaunt/greece.html

Genealogy Societies Online List:
http://www.daddezio.com/catalog/grkndx04.html

German Research Association:
http://feefhs.org/gra/frg-gra.html

Greek Surname Studies and Database Links:
http://www.daddezio.com/catalog/grkndx05.html

Greek Genealogy (Hellenes-Diaspora Greek Genealogy)
https://www.familysearch.org/wiki/en/Greece_Compiled_Genealogies

Greek Genealogy Home Page:
http://www.daddezio.com/grekgen.html

Greek Genealogy Articles:
http://www.daddezio.com/catalog/grkndx01.html

India Genealogy:
http://genforum.genealogy.com/india/

India Family Histories:
http://www.mycinnamontoast.com/perl/results.cgi?region=79&sort=n

India-Anglo-Indian/Europeans in India genealogy:
http://members.ozemail.com.au/~clday/

Irish Travelers:
http://www.pitt.edu/~alkst3/Traveller.html

Japanese Genealogy:
http://www.rootsweb.com/~jpnwgw/

Jewish Genealogy:
http://www.jewishgen.org/infofiles/

Latvian Jewish Genealogy Page:
http://feefhs.org/jsig/frg-lsig.html

Lebanese Genealogy:
http://www.rootsweb.com/~lbnwgw/

Lithuanian American Genealogy Society:
http://feefhs.org/frg-lags.html

Melungeon:
http://www.geocities.com/Paris/5121/melunge
on.htm

Mennonite Heritage Center:
http://feefhs.org/men/frg-mhc.html

Middle East Genealogy:
http://www.rootsweb.com/~mdeastgw/index.h
tml

Middle East Genealogy by country:
http://www.rootsweb.com/~mdeastgw/index.h
tml#country

Native American:
http://www.cyndislist.com/native.htm

Polish Genealogical Society of America:
http://feefhs.org/pol/frg-pgsa.html

Quebec and Francophone:
http://www.francogene.com/quebec/amerin.ht
ml

Romanian American Heritage Center:
http://feefhs.org/ro/frg-rahc.html

Slovak World: http://feefhs.org/slovak/frg-
sw.html

Slavs, South: Cultural Society:
http://feefhs.org/frg-csss.html

Syrian and Lebanese Genealogy:
http://www.genealogytoday.com/family/syrian
/

Syria Genealogy:
http://www.rootsweb.com/~syrwgw/

Tibetan Genealogy:
http://www.distantcousin.com/Links/Ethnic/Chi
na/Tibetan.html

Turkish Genealogy Discussion Group:
http://www.turkey.com/forums/forumdisplay.p
hp3?forumid=18

Ukrainian Genealogical and Historical Society of
Canada: http://feefhs.org/ca/frgughsc.html

Unique Peoples:
http://www.cyndislist.com/peoples.htm. Note:
The Unique People's list includes: Black Dutch,
Doukhobors, Gypsy, Romani, Romany &
Travellers, Melungeons, Metis, Miscellaneous,
and Wends/Sorbs

#

Appendix B:

Genealogy Web sites, (General):

Ancestry.com:
http://www.ancestry.com/main.htm?lfl=m

Cyndi's List of Genealogy on the Internet:
http://www.cyndislist.com/

Cyndi's List is a categorized & cross-referenced index to genealogical resources on the Internet with thousands of links.

DistantCousin.com (Uniting Cousins Worldwide)
http://distantcousin.com/Links/surname.html

Ellis Island Online: http://www.ellisisland.org/

Family History Library:
http://www.familysearch.org/Eng/default.asp

http://www.familysearch.org/Eng/Search/frameset_search.asp

(The Church of Jesus Christ of Latter Day Saints) International Genealogical Index

Female Ancestors:
http://www.cyndislist.com/female.htm

Genealogist's Index to the Web:
http://www.genealogytoday.com/GIWWW/?

Genealogy Web
http://www.genealogyweb.com/

Genealogy Authors and Speakers:
http://feefhs.org/frg/frg-a&l.html

Genealogy Today:
http://www.genealogytoday.com/

My Genealogy.com:
http://www.genealogy.com/cgi-
bin/my_main.cgi

Scriver, Dr. Charles: The Canadian Medical Hall
of Fame
http://www.virtualmuseum.ca/Exhibitions/Med
icentre/en/scri_print.htm

Surname Sites:
http://www.cyndislist.com/surn-gen.htm

National Genealogical Society:
http://www.ngsgenealogy.org/index.htm

United States List of Local by State Genealogical
Societies:
http://www.daddezio.com/society/hill/index.ht
ml

United States Vital Records List:
http://www.daddezio.com/records/room/index
.html or http://www.cyndislist.com/usvital.htm

Appendix C:

**Write Memoirs Using Action Verbs Resource
List: Putting verbs in your sentence.**

Action Verbs

1. Abated

2. Abbreviated

3. Abstracted

4. Abided

5. Abjured

6. Abnegated

7. Abraded

8. Abridged

9. Abrogated

10. Abseiled

11. Absolved

12. Abstained

13. Absorbed

14. Abstracted

15. Abutted

16. Accepted

17. Accelerated

18. Acclaimed

19. Accented

20. Accepted

21. Acclimatized

22. Accommodated

23. Accompanied

24. Accomplished

25. Accorded

26. Accounted

27. Accredited

28. Accrued

29. Accumulated

30. Accustomed

31. Achieved

32. Acknowledged

33. Acquainted

34. Acquiesced

35. Acquired

36. Acquitted

37. Acted

38. Activated

39.   Actualized

40.   Actuated

41.   Adapted

42.   Added

43.   Addressed

44.   Adduced

45.   Adhered

46.   Adjudged

47.   Adjudicated

48.   Adjoined

49.   Adjourned

50.   Adjured

51.   Adjusted

52.   Ad-libbed

53.   Administered

54.   Admired

55.   Admitted

56.   Adopted

57.   Adored

58.   Adorned

59.   Adumbrated

60.   Advanced

61.   Advertised

62.   Advised

63.   Advocated

64.   Aerated

65.   Affected

66.   Affiliated

67.   Affirmed

68.   Affixed

69.   Afforded

70.   Agglutinated

71.   Aggrandized

72.   Agreed

73.   Aided

74.   Aligned

75.   Allied

76.   Allocated

77. Allotted

78. Alternated

79. Amazed

80. Amended

81. Amplified

82. Amused

83. Analyzed

84. Anesthetized

85. Animated

86. Annotated

87. Announced

88. Answered

89. Anticipated

90. Appealed

91. Appeared

92. Appended

93. Appertained (to)

94. Applauded

95. Applied

96.   Appliquéd

97.   Appointed

98.   Appraised

99.   Apprised

100.   Approached

101.   Approved

102.   Approximated

103.   Arbitrated

104.   Archived

105.   Argued

106.   Arose (from)

107.   Arranged

108.   Arrived

109.   Articulated

110.   Ascertained

111.   Ascribed

112.   Aspired

113.   Brought

114.   Budgeted

115.   Built

116.   Calculated

117.   Calmed

118.   Campaigned

119.   Camped

120.   Captivated

121.   Carded

122.   Cared

123.   Carried

124.   Carted

125.   Carved

126.   Catalogued

127.   Catapulted

128.   Centered

129.   Chaired

130.   Changed

131.   Channeled

132.   Characterized

133.   Charged

134.   Charted

135.   Chartered

136.   Cheered

137.   Cherished

138.   Chiseled

139.   Chronicled

140.   Cited

141.   Civilized

142.   Claimed

143.   Clarified

144.   Cleaned

145.   Cleared

146.   Clocked

147.   Closed

148.   Clued

149.   Coached

150.   Coded

151.   Codified

152.   Coifed

153.   Collaborated

154.   Collected

155.   Colored

156.   Comforted

157.   Commanded

158.   Commemorated

159.   Commercialized

160.   Commissioned

161.   Communicated

162.   Compared

163.   Compensated

164.   Competed

165.   Compiled

166.   Complimented

167.   Completed

168.   Composed

169.   Computed

170.   Computerized

171.   Conceived

172. Concentrated

173. Conceptualized

174. Conciliated

175. Concluded

176. Conducted

177. Configured

178. Congratulated

179. Congregated

180. Connected

181. Connoted

182. Conquered

183. Conserved

184. Considered

185. Constructed

186. Construed

187. Consulted

188. Consumed

189. Contracted

190. Continued

191.   Contributed

192.   Controlled

193.   Converged

194.   Conversed

195.   Cooperated

196.   Co-opted

197.   Coordinated

198.   Copyrighted

199.   Corded

200.   Corrected

201.   Correlated

202.   Counseled

203.   Counted

204.   Countered

205.   Courted

206.   Created

207.   Credited

208.   Crewed

209.   Critiqued

210. Crusaded

211. Cued

212. Cultured

213. Curtailed

214. Customized

215. Cut

216. Cycled

217. Dated

218. Dealt

219. Debited

220. Debriefed

221. Debugged

222. Detailed

223. Decentralized

224. Decided

225. Deciphered

226. Declaimed

227. Declared

228. Decoded

229.   Decorated

230.   Decreased

231.   Dedicated

232.   Deferred

233.   Defined

234.   Deflected

235.   Delegated

236.   Deleted

237.   Delighted (in)

238.   Delineated

239.   Delivered

240.   Demonstrated

241.   Demystified

242.   Denominate

243.   Denoted

244.   Depicted

245.   Deprogrammed

246.   Deregulated

247.   Derived

248.   Described

249.   Designed

250.   Detailed

251.   Detected

252.   Determined

253.   Detoured

254.   Developed

255.   Devised

256.   Devolved

257.   Dined

258.   Disclosed

259.   Dithered

260.   Divided

261.   Divulged

262.   Delighted

263.   Derived

264.   Devised

265.   Devoted

266.   Diagnosed

267.   Dialogued

268.   Diced

269.   Dichotomized

270.   Dictated

271.   Differed

272.   Digested

273.   Digitized

274.   Diluted

275.   Directed

276.   Digitized

277.   Disagreed

278.   Disclosed

279.   Discovered

280.   Discussed

281.   Dispatched

282.   Dispersed

283.   Displayed

284.   Dissolved

285.   Distributed

286. Diversified

287. Divided

288. Divined

289. Documented

290. Docked

291. Donated

292. Doused

293. Drafted

294. Drew

295. Drove

296. Earned

297. Edited

298. Editorialized

299. Educated

300. Effected

301. Effloresced

302. Eked out

303. Elaborated

304. Elasticized

305. Elbowed

306. Elected

307. Elegized

308. Elevated

309. Eliminated

310. Embroidered

311. Emended

312. Emote

313. Emphasized

314. Employed

315. Empowered

316. Encased

317. Encountered

318. Encouraged

319. Energized

320. Engaged

321. Engineered

322. Engraved

323. Enhanced

324.   Enlarged

325.   Enlightened

326.   Enlisted

327.   Enlivened

328.   Enriched

329.   Ensconced

330.   Ensured

331.   Entered

332.   Entertained

333.   Envisioned

334.   Epigrammatized

335.   Epitomized

336.   Equalized

337.   Erected

338.   Eructed

339.   Escorted

340.   Established

341.   Estimated

342.   Etched

343.	Etiolated

344.	Eulogized

345.	Euphemized

346.	Evaluated

347.	Evanesced

348.	Evangelized

349.	Evidenced

350.	Evoked

351.	Evolved

352.	Exacerbated

353.	Exacted

354.	Exalted

355.	Examined

356.	Excavated

357.	Excelled

358.	Exchanged

359.	Exclaimed

360.	Excoriated

361.	Exculpated

362. Executed

363. Exemplified

364. Exercised

365. Exhorted

366. Exfoliated

367. Exhibited

368. Exonerated

369. Exorcized

370. Expanded

371. Expatiated

372. Expedited

373. Experienced

374. Explained

375. Explored

376. Exported

377. Exposed

378. Expressed

379. Extended

380. Extolled

381.   Extrapolated

382.   Facilitated

383.   Farmed

384.   Fascinated

385.   Fastened

386.   Faxed

387.   Fed

388.   Federalized

389.   Felicitated

390.   Ferreted

391.   Fertilized

392.   Fetched

393.   Fictionalized

394.   Filed

395.   Filled

396.   Filmed

397.   Financed

398.   Fired

399.   Fitted

400.	Fixed

401.	Flattered

402.	Flew

403.	Flaunted

404.	Flourished

405.	Fluctuated

406.	Flummoxed

407.	Followed

408.	Forecasted

409.	Formalized

410.	Formatted

411.	Formed

412.	Formulated

413.	Fortified

414.	Forwarded

415.	Found

416.	Founded

417.	Franchised

418.	Fraternized

419.   Freed

420.   Froze

421.   Fulfilled

422.   Functioned

423.   Furnished

424.   Gained

425.   Garnished

426.   Gathered

427.   Gave

428.   Generated

429.   Genealogized

430.   Geneticized

431.   Genuflected

432.   Gestured

433.   Gesticulated

434.   Girded

435.   Glorified

436.   Gnosticized

437.   Governed

438. Graded

439. Grafted

440. Granted

441. Graphed

442. Gratified

443. Greeted

444. Grew

445. Guaranteed

446. Guarded

447. Guided

448. Hafted

449. Hailed

450. Halted

451. Handled

452. Harbored

453. Harmonized

454. Hastened

455. Harvested

456. Headed

457.   Healed

458.   Heaped

459.   Heard

460.   Heated

461.   Helped

462.   Hewed

463.   Hired

464.   Honored

465.   Hoped

466.   Hosted

467.   Hugged

468.   Humanized

469.   Humored

470.   Hustled

471.   Hypnotized

472.   Hypothesized

473.   Identified

474.   Ignited

475.   Illustrated

476.   Immigrated

477.   Implanted

478.   Implemented

479.   Implied

480.   Imported

481.   Imposed

482.   Impressed

483.   Improved

484.   Incited

485.   Included

486.   Incorporated

487.   Increased

488.   Indexed

489.   Indicated

490.   Indicted

491.   Indulged

492.   Industrialized

493.   Influenced

494.   Informed

495.   Initialized

496.   Initiated

497.   Inked

498.   Inquired

499.   Inspected

500.   Inspired

501.   Installed

502.   Instituted

503.   Instructed

504.   Insured

505.   Integrated

506.   Interested

507.   Interfaced

508.   Internalized

509.   Internationalized

510.   Interpreted

511.   Interviewed

512.   Introduced

513.   Intuited

514.   Invested

515.   Investigated

516.   Invented

517.   Inventoried

518.   Inverted

519.   Invested

520.   Invigorated

521.   Involved

522.   Issued

523.   Joined

524.   Journalized

525.   Journeyed

526.   Judged

527.   Juried

528.   Justified

529.   Juxtaposed

530.   Keyboarded

531.   Lamented

532.   Laminated

533.   Landed (in)

534.   Landscaped

535.   Leased

536.   Launched

537.   Lectured

538.   Legalized

539.   Legitimized

540.   Legislated

541.   Lessened

542.   Led

543.   Left

544.   Lighted

545.   Linked

546.   Listened

547.   Litigated

548.   Loaded

549.   Loaned

550.   Lobbied

551.   Localized

552. Looked

553. Lyricized

554. Magnetized

555. Mailed

556. Maintained

557. Managed

558. Manipulated

559. Manufactured

560. Marked

561. Marketed

562. Mastered

563. Measured

564. Mediated

565. Memorized

566. Mentored

567. Merchandised

568. Merged

569. Met

570. Micrographed

571.   Migrated

572.   Ministered

573.   Moderated

574.   Modified

575.   Modeled

576.   Molded

577.   Monitored

578.   Morphed

579.   Mortgaged

580.   Motivated

581.   Moved

582.   Multiplied

583.   Multitasked

584.   Narrated

585.   Navigated

586.   Negotiated

587.   Networked

588.   Neutered

589.   Neutralized

590.   Normalized

591.   Normed

592.   Notated

593.   Noted

594.   Notified

595.   Notarized

596.   Nourished

597.   Nursed

598.   Obtained

599.   Officiated

600.   Opened

601.   Orated

602.   Operated

603.   Opined

604.   Orchestrated

605.   Ordered

606.   Organized

607.   Oriented

608.   Originated

609.   Outlaid

610.   Outlined

611.   Outnumbered

612.   Outpaced

613.   Outperformed

614.   Outplayed

615.   Outran

616.   Outshone

617.   Outranked

618.   Outvoted

619.   Outwitted

620.   Overawed

621.   Overcame

622.   Overdid

623.   Overheard

624.   Oversaw

625.   Overstepped

626.   Overstretched

627.   Overwhelmed

628. Overworked

629. Overwrote

630. Owed

631. Owned

632. Oxygenated

633. Oxidized

634. Paced

635. Packaged

636. Packed

637. Parented

638. Participated

639. Partnered (with)

640. Patented

641. Patterned

642. Perceived

643. Perfected

644. Performed

645. Persevered

646. Persisted

647.	Personalized

648.	Persuaded

649.	Perused

650.	Petitioned

651.	Photocopied

652.	Photographed

653.	Piloted

654.	Pinpointed

655.	Pitched

656.	Placed

657.	Planned

658.	Planted

659.	Played

660.	Plotted

661.	Pooled

662.	Posed

663.	Posted

664.	Positioned

665.	Practiced

666.   Praised

667.   Prayed

668.   Predicted

669.   Preempted

670.   Prefaced

671.   Preferred

672.   Prepared

673.   Presented

674.   Presided

675.   Pressed

676.   Prevented

677.   Probed

678.   Proceeded (to)

679.   Processed

680.   Procreated

681.   Procured

682.   Produced

683.   Professionalized

684.   Programmed

685.	Projected

686.	Promulgated

687.	Promoted

688.	Proposed

689.	Proscribed

690.	Proofread

691.	Prospered

692.	Protected

693.	Protested

694.	Protracted

695.	Proved

696.	Provided

697.	Publicized

698.	Published

699.	Purchased

700.	Pursued

701.	Qualified

702.	Quantified

703.	Quickened

704.   Questioned

705.   Queued

706.   Quilted

707.   Raised

708.   Ran

709.   Ranged

710.   Rated

711.   Razed

712.   Reached

713.   Realized

714.   Reaped

715.   Rearranged

716.   Reared

717.   Reasoned

718.   Recalled

719.   Recited

720.   Received

721.   Recited

722.   Reclaimed

723.   Recognized

724.   Recommended

725.   Reconciled

726.   Reconstructed

727.   Recorded

728.   Recouped

729.   Recovered

730.   Recreated

731.   Recruited

732.   Rectified

733.   Recycled

734.   Redesigned

735.   Redecorated

736.   Redistricted

737.   Reduced

738.   Reenacted

739.   Reentered

740.   Referenced

741.   Refreshed

742.   Registered

743.   Regulated

744.   Rehearsed

745.   Rehired

746.   Reimbursed

747.   Reinforced

748.   Rejoiced

749.   Related

750.   Released

751.   Relinquished

752.   Relocated

753.   Remedied

754.   Reminisced

755.   Remembered

756.   Remodeled

757.   Renewed

758.   Rented

759.   Reoriented

760.   Repaired

761.   Replenished

762.   Replied

763.   Reported

764.   Reposed

765.   Represented

766.   Requested

767.   Required

768.   Requisitioned

769.   Researched

770.   Resized

771.   Reshaped

772.   Resolved

773.   Responded to

774.   Restored

775.   Resourced

776.   Resulted

777.   Retailed

778.   Retained

779.   Retrained

780.   Retired

781.   Retooled

782.   Retorted

783.   Retrained

784.   Retrieved

785.   Returned

786.   Reunited

787.   Revamped

788.   Reveled

789.   Reviewed

790.   Revised

791.   Revived

792.   Rewired

793.   Roboticized

794.   Rolled

795.   Rose

796.   Rotated

797.   Routed

798.   Rushed

799.   Sailed

800.   Sampled

801.   Sanitized

802.   Saved

803.   Scanned

804.   Scheduled

805.   Scored

806.   Screened

807.   Scrimped

808.   Sculptured

809.   Secured

810.   Sequenced

811.   Selected

812.   Sensed

813.   Serialized

814.   Served

815.   Set objectives

816.   Set up

817.   Sewed

818.   Shaped

819.   Shared

820.   Shredded

821.   Showed

822.   Signified

823.   Simplified

824.   Sized

825.   Skilled

826.   Socialized

827.   Sold

828.   Solicited

829.   Solidified

830.   Solved

831.   Sorted

832.   Sought

833.   Spared

834.   Sparked

835.   Spayed

836.   Specified

837.   Speculated

838.   Spiced

839.   Spirited

840.   Spoke

841.   Sponsored

842.   Spread

843.   Staffed

844.   Stabilized

845.   Standardized

846.   Starred

847.   Stated

848.   Stepped

849.   Sterilized

850.   Stimulated

851.   Stored

852.   Straightened

853.   Streamlined

854.   Strengthened

855.   Stretched

856.   Strolled

857.   Strove

858.   Structured

859.   Styled

860.   Subcontracted

861.   Submitted

862.   Succeeded

863.   Summarized

864.   Supervised

865.   Supplied

866.   Supported

867.   Surfed

868.   Surmised

869.   Surveyed

870.   Survived

871.   Syndicated

872.   Synthesized

873.   Systematized

874.   Tabulated

875.   Tamped

876.   Taught

877.   Taxed

878.   Teamed (up)

879.   Telecommuted

880.   Telemarketed

881.   Telephoned

882.   Televised

883.   Terminated

884.   Tested

885.   Thwarted

886.   Told

887.   Tolled

888.   Toughened

889.   Toured

890.   Traced

891.   Tracked

892.   Traded

893.   Trained

894.   Transacted

895.   Transcribed

896.   Transferred

897.   Translated

898.   Transmitted

899.   Transported

900.   Traveled

901.   Treated

902.   Trekked

903.   Triumphed

904.   Troubleshot

905.   Trucked

906.   Truncated

907.   Trusted

908.   Turned

909.   Typed

910.   Typeset

911.   Understood

912.   Undertook

913. Unified

914. United

915. Updated

916. Upgraded

917. Uplifted

918. Underscored

919. Used

920. Utilized

921. Validated

922. Valued

923. Varied

924. Vaunted

925. Venerated

926. Ventured

927. Verbalized

928. Verified

929. Video recorded

930. Viewed

931. Vindicated

932.   Visualized

933.   Vitalized

934.   Vocalized

935.   Voiced

936.   Volunteered

937.   Voted

938.   Vulcanized

939.   Waited

940.   Waived

941.   Watched

942.   Waved

943.   Weaned

944.   Weighed

945.   Weighted

946.   Welded

947.   Willed

948.   Wintered

949.   Withdrew

950.   Wholesaled

951.   Won

952.   Word processed

953.   Worked

954.   Wrote

955.   Wrought

956.   Xerographed

957.   X-rayed

958.   Yearned

959.   Yielded

960.   Zapped

961.   Zested

962.   Zigzagged

963.   Zipped

964.   Zeroed (in)

965.   Zoomed

966.   Zoned

967.   Zzz (slang: verb, "sawed wood")

#

www.ingramcontent.com/pod-product-compliance
Lightning Source LLC
Chambersburg PA
CBHW070108260726
48658CB00001B/32